WORLD WIDE INVESTOR

Risks, Rewards and Opportunities for the Astute Investor

William J. Corney
Leonard E. Goodall

PROBUS PUBLISHING COMPANY
Chicago, Illinois

This publication is designed to provide accurate and authoritative information in regard to the subject matter covered. It is sold with the understanding that the publisher is not engaged in rendering legal, accounting or other professional service. If legal or other expert assistance is required, the services of a competent professional should be sought.

Library of Congress Cataloging in Publication Data Available.

ISBN   1-55738-205-0

Printed in the United States of America

KP

1   2   3   4   5   6   7   8   9   0

CONTENTS

PREFACE

Only once in the past decade was the U.S. market among the top five performing markets in the world. Moreover, for the greater part of the decade, most world currencies have appreciated against the dollar, boosting the U.S. dollar value of all types of foreign investments. No longer can we assume that America is the best investment bet; for the individual investor to ignore world markets as we approach the 21st century is shortsighted.

The goal of this book is to provide you with the background necessary to become an astute global investor. We hope the *Worldwide Investor* will be valuable to both beginning and seasoned investors alike.

You will learn from this book the basic principles for successful global investing. You will also learn how the international banking system can be of benefit to you. You'll be exposed to information about the three investment "super regions" of the world: North America, the Asian Pacific Basin, and Greater Europe. You will learn how to invest safely through dollar averaging, asset allocation, and market timing. Finally, you will learn about the opportunities and benefits in owning foreign real estate. In short, the *Worldwide Investor* will show you how to profit from the exciting period of world growth that lies before us.

William J. Corney
Leonard E. Goodall

CHAPTER 1

Financial Planning in a Global Economy

One of the most important financial trends of recent years has been the globalization of economies. It is hardly realistic today to speak of the U.S. economy or the Japanese or Asian economies. The financial affairs of each country and region affect economic trends everywhere. If interest rates go up in Europe, money will be withdrawn from U.S. security markets and moved to those European investments which will provide a higher return. If the Japanese quit buying U.S. Treasury bonds, it will be more difficult to finance our national debt and interest rates will rise. That will make it harder to borrow money for a new house, new car or for business purposes.

The globalization of economies provides both opportunities and dangers for the individual investor. An individual can now invest in virtually any specific part of the world, and an investment portfolio can be diversified geographically as well as in other ways. It is also possible to maintain bank accounts or certificates of deposit in any of several currencies, not just in the currency of one's own country.

Despite the opportunities, globalization brings with it several types of potential pitfalls. It is usually harder to get information about foreign stocks and bonds than about those which trade in the

1

United States. Securities exchanges in other nations are often less tightly regulated than are U.S. exchanges. Moreover, the volatility of many currencies makes uncertainty about monetary exchange rates one more element of risk when making investments in other nations.

In spite of problems, international investing is, and will remain, an important and necessary fact of life for the individual investor. In the past, the average investor would have been unlikely to say, "I am only going to invest in the stock of companies in my home state." The investor looking forward to the twenty-first century will be equally unlikely to consider only investment opportunities in his or her own country.

Before "jumping-in" to the global investment arena, it is important to pause and take a hard look at your financial situation. International investment success requires a balancing of risk and potential return, within the framework of your long term goals. Personal financial planning is the key to developing this strategic balance.

PERSONAL FINANCIAL PLANNING

Personal financial planning is a process of analyzing one's financial situation, establishing long-range financial goals and identifying the necessary steps for achieving those goals. The planning process should include the following steps:

A. Taking a financial inventory
B. Assessing your personal situation
C. Establishing long range goals
D. Providing for immediate needs
E. Establishing an investment strategy
F. Monitoring and reviewing financial status

Taking a Financial Inventory

The first step in the financial planning process is knowing your current financial status. This involves identifying everything you own and determining the total value of all your assets. Then you will identify all your debts (mortgage, car loan, credit card debt, etc.) to determine your total indebtedness. By subtracting your total debts from your assets you will then be able to determine your financial net worth.

Table 1-1 is an example of how a typical family's statement of net worth might look. You will notice that assets are divided into two categories, *use* assets and *investment* assets. In most cases it will be obvious which assets go where. Sometimes it will be a matter of personal preference. Note that John and Mary Saver have a coin collection which they list as a use asset. This is because coin collecting is their hobby; they buy coins for enjoyment and have no intention of selling them. If they bought coins primarily as part of an investment strategy, they might choose to list them under investment assets.

A statement of net worth is used for more reasons than just determining a family's total financial holdings. An important function of the statement is assisting in the analysis of one's asset diversification. The family's investment assets are divided into five categories:

- Equities
- Bonds
- Cash and cash equivalents
- Real estate
- Precious metals

Arranging the assets in this manner provides a clear view of how well one's investments are diversified. As we will discuss often throughout the book, diversification is the single most important investment principle for the average individual investor.

The investor can also use the financial statement to review the geographic distribution of a portfolio. For example, we see in Table 1-1 that the family has made several global investments. They own a mutual fund that invests in Asian stocks, 50 shares in a Japanese bank stock and some Canadian gold coins. Their other investments, a growth mutual fund, municipal bond fund, and others, are U. S. investments. It is very likely today, however, that a U.S. based growth mutual fund might well have some of its funds invested in stocks of foreign companies.

Table 1-1 Statement of Net Worth

John and Mary Saver
123 Thrifty Street
Security Village, USA

Use Assets		Debts	
Auto I	$ 8,000	Mortgage	$45,200
Auto II	4,000	Credit Cards	1,400
House	150,000	Auto I Loan	3,000
Furniture	20,000	Total Debts	$49,600
Personal Items	10,000		
Boat	8,000		
Stamp Collection	4,000		
Total Use Assets	$204,000		
Investment Assets		Net Worth	
Equities		(Total assets	
U.S. Growth Fund	8,100	Less debt)	$199,600
Asian Mutual Fund	3,200		
100 Sh Gen. Mot.	4,300		
50 Sh Fukiyama Bank	6,300		
	$ 21,900 48.5%		
Bonds			
Muni. Bond Fund	$ 5,300 11.7%		
Cash and Cash Equivalents			
Checking Account	$ 2,000		
Certi. of Deposit	8,000		
Life Ins. Cash Val.	1,000		
	$ 11,000 24.3%		
Real Estate			
Limited Partnership	$ 5,000 11.1%		
Precious Metals			
Canadian Gold Coins	$ 2,000 4.4%		
Total Investment Assets	$ 45,200 100.0%		
		Total Debts	
Total Assets	$249,200	and Net Worth	$249,200

Let us look more closely at their foreign investments. They break down geographically as follows:

Asia:	Asian Mutual Fund
	Fukiyama Bank
North America:	Canadian gold coins
Central and South America:	None
Europe:	None

What does this pattern of diversification imply? It *may* mean that they have made a deliberate decision to emphasize Asian investments. Perhaps they are convinced that the Pacific Rim countries of Asia are "where the action is" and where profits can best be made in the next several years.

It also may simply mean that they haven't thought much about their investments in geographical terms. If that is the case, they may want to consider making their next investment in a mutual fund that invests in the stocks of European funds. Alternatively, they could buy a global fund, which invests in a diversified portfolio of stocks from all parts of the world.

Assessing Your Personal Situation

The statement of net worth, therefore, can be used to review different types of diversification, by geography as well as by type of investment. This preparation of a financial inventory is the first step in the financial planning process.

A financial inventory tells us only part of what we need to know in our financial planning. Each individual and family has its own set of personal circumstances which will impact on financial planning decisions. An individual who knows he will inherit one million dollars in a few years has very different financial needs than the person who has a physically handicapped daughter whom he will have to help support throughout her life.

Children have very different financial needs in so far as education is concerned. If you have a daughter who wants to be a physician and a son who wants to be an auto mechanic, the cost of providing each of them with the necessary education will vary greatly.

A couple who are both well-paid professionals will plan financial matters differently than the couple who want the wife (or maybe the husband) to stay at home and not work.

In this area, the global orientation of individuals can make a difference. Many people have relatives in foreign countries and return to visit them on a regular basis. Some families are able to spend their winters on the French Riviera, in the Bahamas or on the coast of Mexico. There are others who make a shopping trip to Hong Kong every year. Many people have to travel overseas as part of their business activities. Such travel patterns may make you aware of investment opportunities. Seeing a McDonald's in Tokyo or being able to buy a Pepsi in Moscow might have given an observant traveler back in the 1970's a clue about a good investment back home.

A person who travels regularly to Switzerland to ski may want to keep a bank account there. The "little guy" investor who does not do much traveling but who lives near the Canadian border may want to watch interest rates and investment opportunities across the border and perhaps invest a portion of his resources there. The Mexican economy has made a good comeback in recent years, and the resident of San Diego or El Paso is in a good position to watch developments there closely and take advantage of investment opportunities.

Establishing Long Range Goals

After analyzing one's financial inventory and personal financial situation, the next step is to establish long range goals. For many individuals and families these would include:

- Buying a home
- Starting a business
- Paying for children's education
- Providing for retirement

As the retirement age gets closer, an individual should begin to think about specific goals that would come under the general heading of providing for retirement. These retirement goals should include, at least, the following:

- Providing current income
- Protecting against inflation
- Providing for health and long-term care needs
- Preparing estate distribution plans

For some people other specific retirement goals might include paying off the mortgage, buying a retirement condominium or starting a new part-time business after retirement.

Providing for current income is usually the first priority for most of us at the time of retirement. There was a time when it was considered that an amount equal to two-thirds of pre-retirement income would be a sufficient income during retirement. Concerns about inflation and longer life spans have changed this, and today most financial planners would suggest an amount equal to 75 percent to 80 percent of pre-retirement income is a better objective. This will usually come from a combination of several sources, including social security, private pensions, and savings and investments.

Inflation protection is a more difficult goal to achieve. The first problem is that it is impossible to predict future inflation rates. Since many people now live twenty years or more beyond retirement, inflation projections are at best "guesstimates" about the future. Some pension plans today provide options that allow for annual inflation adjustments, and it is also possible to buy annuities that will provide annual increases in income.

Individuals retiring early must be especially sensitive to the inflation question. First, the reduction in pension benefits when a person takes early retirement is often significant. For example, a worker who begins receiving social security payments at age 62 will receive 20 percent less in monthly benefits than the worker who retires at age 65. Private pensions often have similar provisions. Also, the earlier one retires, the harder it becomes to make the long-range projections of inflation rates throughout the individual's life expectancy.

The individual with an international aspect to his or her retirement plans may need to consider costs of living and inflation rates in various regions of the world. Many U.S. citizens have moved to small communities in Mexico to retire, and they have found they can live comfortably on a minimal income. On the other hand, many residents of England and Scandinavia have moved to the southern coast of Spain to retire. They have found that the very fact of many Northern Europeans moving there to retire has itself been a factor in pushing up living costs. If an individual plans to retire in one country, perhaps Mexico or Spain, and keep an investment portfolio in another, perhaps the U.S. or Switzerland, that intensifies the need to consider future inflation rates in all the areas involved.

Many people today would argue that no aspect of retirement planning is more critical than assuring that one's health and long-term care plans are provided for. A long stay in a hospital for someone without health insurance can wipe out a middle class family's entire savings. Medicare and Medicaid will be of help to many, but most of us will need some type of health insurance to help protect us from the financial disaster that often accompanies an accident or long-term illness. Likewise, if the time comes when one must live in a retirement home of some type, that can be very costly if it has not been planned for ahead of time.

The best time to provide for health and care costs is often in the years just before retirement. Some workers have the option of taking advantage of the group insurance plans of their employers and then keeping the plans after retirement. Even if the worker has to carry part or all of the costs after retirement, this may still be the best alternative. On this point also, a retiree may have an international aspect to consider. If you are planning to retire in a foreign country, check into what types of health care you may qualify for as a resident. Some countries with national health care systems may provide you with services you would have to pay for in the U.S. There is no need to buy insurance to cover medical services you will receive free in your new country of residence.

Finally, most of us will want to plan for the final distribution of our assets after our death. We may ensure that if we do not make such plans, the government will do it for us. Each state has laws directing how one's assets will be distributed for those who die without having a will. Most of us would rather do it ourselves.

Estate planning can involve actions that occur before death. Money that we give away to heirs or to charitable organizations during our lives is money that will not have to be distributed after death. Many individuals are surprised at how much they are worth (one reason for the financial inventory) and therefore how important estate planning can be. Such planning may involve wills, trusts, charitable giving plans, etc.

One point worth keeping in mind is that different countries and even different states each have their own laws on these matters. If you own financial assets in various locations, it is very likely that more than one jurisdiction will attempt to levy gift, estate or inheritance taxes against your estate. Look into this matter carefully and be sure, with the help of your attorney or accountant, that you know the likely implications of owning assets in various places.

The subject of estate planning is complex, and we cannot cover it adequately here. Suffice it to say that no family's financial planning is complete if it does not cover estate planning.

Providing for Current Needs

After assessing one's personal situation and establishing long-term goals, the individual must begin the process of implementing the plans. Implementation should begin with providing for immediate needs. Some people set very detailed budgets and adhere strictly to them. Others are much more general in their budgeting. There are good books on personal budgeting, and we will not attempt to cover that subject in detail here.

We would just remind you here of several items that should be included in meeting immediate needs. Food, clothing and housing must be part of any budget. There are no hard and fast rules for budgeting for these. Financial planners used to suggest that about 25 percent of one's income could reasonably be spent for housing. Today many people must spend more than that. In some areas, New York and San Francisco for example, it is not uncommon to spend nearly half of one's income on housing costs.

An individual or family's current needs should include adequate insurance. This will usually include life and health insurance, auto, disability and often an umbrella policy to provide protection against liability charges. Insurance is a subject that deserves careful attention. Most people will want to do some homework on their own and probably get some professional assistance to help decide on an adequate and balanced insurance program.

Another important part of providing for current needs is to have an emergency fund in case of an unexpected loss of income. A serious illness, accident or sudden loss of job can create a financial emergency. Most students of family budgets recommend an amount of two to six months of living expenses should be set aside for this purpose. Your own job situation will help determine what is adequate for you. If you are a teacher with tenure or a worker protected with many years of seniority, an amount equal to two months of your living expenses might be adequate. If you are in a job position that you have a high probability of losing, either permanently or temporarily, you may want to keep an amount equal to five or six month's of expenses set aside.

Providing for a possible emergency does not mean keeping that money in your checking account, but it should be where it is available on short notice. The funds might be kept in a savings account, money market account or short-term certificate of deposit. You might think of the cash value of your life insurance policy as part of your emergency fund since it is usually accessible on relatively short notice.

For some people, immediate needs may involve overseas needs. The individual who is in Tokyo on business several times a year or who spends several weeks every summer on the southern coast of France should consider keeping a bank account in that location. It might also be wise to keep the account in the local currency. This prevents having to worry about frequent fluctuation in currency valuations. Since you will regularly be spending money in the local currency, it makes sense to have it available without having to worry about its value in relation to the value of your home country currency. The uses of foreign bank accounts will be discussed more in Chapter Three.

Developing an Investment Strategy

After an individual has completed the steps described above, it is time to develop a personal investment strategy, or perhaps more than one strategy. This involves understanding one's own abilities, preferences and levels of risk tolerance.

How much risk will you tolerate? Are there some kinds of investments that cause you to lie awake and worry at night? These are the types of questions it is essential to consider. The answers are different for each individual. Generally, older investors should accept less risk than younger ones. Higher income individuals can often take more risk, at least with part of their investment funds, than those who must devote nearly all their income to meeting current needs. Some individuals may want to take most of their savings and invest them on the basis of a "moderate risk strategy" while devoting a smaller portion of savings (maybe 10 percent or 15 percent) to a "high risk strategy." Chapters Seven through Nine discuss various investment strategies and explain how they can be adjusted to the level of risk tolerance of each individual.

A question closely related to risk tolerance is that of risk preference. Some people can tolerate some types of risk much more easily than others. One may be able to watch the stock market fluctuate wildly without ever getting unduly concerned. That same individual may worry greatly about real estate investments, fretting about vacancies in apartments or worrying that tenants will damage property. Concerns about foreign investments can be especially acute. It is more difficult to get information about stocks and bonds issued in foreign countries, and investment in overseas real estate presents many legal problems as well as the usual problems of owning property at a distance where it cannot be personally supervised on a regular basis.

One's personal abilities and preferences will also enter into the development of investment strategies. The person who understands balance sheets and corporate management has a head start in investing in the stock market. An individual who is skilled in such things as carpentry, plumbing and electrical matters is better prepared than others to get involved in the personal ownership and management of real estate investments. An investor who speaks a foreign language can read newspapers and perhaps even listen to news reports in that language. This gives that person a great advantage in understanding economic and political trends and investment opportunities in countries where that language is spoken.

An individual's personal preferences are also important. A person may have a good understanding of corporate finances, an ability to use a personal computer and access to much information about the stock market. That same person may prefer to spend his spare time on the golf course! He has the ability to develop a sophisticated investment strategy involving the stock market, but he simply prefers not to do so. There is absolutely nothing wrong with this attitude so long as the individual understands it and allows for it.

A good dose of "self analysis" can be a very helpful step in the development of a global investment strategy or strategies. An understanding of one's own risk tolerance, risk preferences and personal abilities and preferences is a good first step in selecting an appropriate investment strategy.

Monitoring and Reviewing

Whatever investment plan you choose will not work on automatic pilot. A wise investor will have a system for reviewing his or her investments on a regular basis. For most investors, a semi-annual or even an annual review is adequate. This should include consideration of such questions as whether individual goals have changed. Once all the children are out of college or the mortgage is paid off it is likely that goals will change. A retirement, change of job or an accident that causes loss of income will necessitate a review of goals.

It is imperative also to review the investments themselves. A decision to have 80 percent of one's investments in stocks may be desirable for a high income 35 year old. At some point, as that individual gets older, it will probably be desirable to reduce the portion of investment funds devoted to stocks. Changes in economic conditions may also lead to a decision to alter one's allocation of investment assets. If the time has come to spend more time on the tennis court or the golf course, it may be time to sell the real estate that takes personal management time and invest the funds in more passive investments that require less time and personal attention.

A global investor will consider economic conditions around the world when reviewing investments. Prior to 1989 no one would have given much thought to investing in eastern Europe. Your personal view today may be that Asia is the place to invest, but over a period of time you may decide that Asian investments have become overpriced and you will change your emphasis to some other area. A businessman who travels regularly to Hong Kong may take advantage of investment opportunities there. If he moves to another job that does not involve overseas travel, he might decide to reduce his investments in Hong Kong, not because they are necessarily bad but because he has less opportunity to personally monitor them.

As noted previously, most of our investments will be in one of five investment areas—equities (stocks), bonds, cash and cash equivalents, real estate and precious metals. A good investment strategy will have objectives for diversifying into several of these categories. The regular review should consider whether that diversification is still appropriate or should be revised. Later chapters provide more help in identifying appropriate investments and developing investment strategies that fit them.

REFERENCES

Block, Stanley, Peavy, John, and Thornton, John. *Personal Financial Management*, (New York, NY: Harper & Row, 1988).

Brosterman, Robert, *The Complete Estate Planning Guide* (New York, NY: McGraw-Hill, 1982).

Gitman, Lawerence, *Personal Financial Planning* (Chicago, IL: Dryden Press, 1987).

Vicker, Ray, *The Dow Jones-Irwin Guide to Retirement Planning* (Homewood, IL: Dow Jones-Irwin, 1987).

CHAPTER 2

Seven Principles for Developing a Successful Global Investment Strategy

To be successful over the long-term you need an investment philosophy that is based on sound principles. This is of special importance to the global investor who is faced with an array of possible investments in an uncertain environment. For many investors, an investment portfolio accrues over the years without any overall planning. A stock may be purchased based on a tip by a co-worker, a bond mutual fund added to the portfolio after reading a magazine article and OEX options may be traded after hearing them touted on a television program. Such haphazard investing without an overall plan of action is a prescription for average to dismal investment performance.

Beyond the enhancement of monetary results, there are other reasons that you may want to establish a rational plan for your investments. Your investment account not only has an important impact on your life when the money is needed for a specific purpose, but it can also affect you long before the money is actually needed. Relatively large accumulations of monetary assets make many people very nervous, especially when the total value fluctuates and control is lacking. The status of investments can therefore have a major psychological impact, even to the point of affecting mood and sleep patterns. The development of a portfolio based on sound principles can reduce the frustrations and feelings of helplessness that arise when times are bad.

PRINCIPLE 1: PLAN FOR LONG-TERM GAINS

Over the span of a few hours to a few days financial markets can be extremely volatile. It is very tempting to think that you may be able to "catch" every short-term rise and fall in prices, thereby amassing a large accumulation of money in a short period of time. In truth, no one has been able to do this consistently despite the heroic efforts of many hopeful speculators over decades. At present, the best model of short-term market movements is randomness, which defies prediction. A more realistic approach to take is to try to match your investment money flows with the major longer-term price swings instead of the short ones. Focus your efforts on movements that you expect to last from many months to years instead of from days to weeks. These are the movements that will offer you the best opportunity to make profits.

Additional support to the long-term view of investing comes from the power of compounding. It has been said that someone once asked Albert Einstein what he thought was the most important invention ever made by man. Dr. Einstein is reported to have said, "Compound interest!" The power of compounding can best be appreciated by comparing ending sums of money at different interest rates. If you could increase your rate of return just a few percentage points per year, on average, over a long period of time, a large increase in the ending balance would result. Table 2-1 shows how compounding at slightly higher rates for a fixed sum of dollars can greatly affect an ending sum.

Let's say, for example, that you decide to actively manage just $10,000 of your investment accumulations and are able to increase the return four percentage points. If you compare the ending balance based on an eight percent return to that of a 12 percent return, you can see a large difference. Over 30 years the balances would be $100,630 at the eight percent rate, but $299,600 at the 12 percent rate!

Figure 2-1 The Effects of Higher Interest Rates On Ending Balances

Values of a Single $10,000 investment at
Given Compound Rates for Years Shown

Investment Horizon (years)	8 percent	12 percent	16 percent	20 percent
5	$14,693	$17,623	$21,003	$24,883
10	21,589	31,058	44,114	61,917
15	31,722	54,736	92,655	154,070
20	46,610	96,463	194,461	383,380
25	68,485	170,000	408,740	953,660
30	100,630	299,600	858,500	2,273,800

Another way to demonstrate the power of compounding is by comparing investment strategies used by two hypothetical investors over a long period of time. Table 2-1 shows the results of investor "X" who started investing $2,000 each year at age 19 for seven years, then quit investing after age 25. Investor "Y" began making investments totaling $2,000 each year starting at age 26 and continued until age 65. If we assume that investments were made at the beginning of each year and a 10 percent annual return was obtained, which investor would have the most money accumulated at age 65?

The table shows the surprising result that the investor X, who had made investments for only seven years, accumulated more money than investor Y, who made investments from age 26 until age 65! The power of compounding tells us that the best time to start investing is NOW. If you have small children or grandchildren, a small gift now, compounded over their working lifetimes, will result in a substantial ending balance.

Table 2-1 Periodic Investments and the Power of Compounding

	Investor X		Investor Y
Age	Amount Invested	Age	Amount Invested
19	$2,000	19	0
20	$2,000	20	0
21	$2,000	21	0
22	$2,000	22	0
23	$2,000	23	0
24	$2,000	24	0
25	$2,000	25	0
26	0	26	$2,000
27	0	27	$2,000
28	0	28	$2,000
29	0	29	$2,000
30	0	30	$2,000
31	0	31	$2,000
32	0	32	$2,000
33	0	33	$2,000
34	0	34	$2,000
35	0	35	$2,000
36	0	36	$2,000
37	0	37	$2,000
38	0	38	$2,000
39	0	39	$2,000
40	0	40	$2,000
41	0	41	$2,000
42	0	42	$2,000
43	0	43	$2,000
44	0	44	$2,000
45	0	45	$2,000
46	0	46	$2,000
47	0	47	$2,000
48	0	48	$2,000
49	0	49	$2,000
50	0	50	$2,000
51	0	51	$2,000
52	0	52	$2,000
53	0	53	$2,000
54	0	54	$2,000
55	0	55	$2,000
56	0	56	$2,000
57	0	57	$2,000
58	0	58	$2,000
59	0	59	$2,000
60	0	60	$2,000
61	0	61	$2,000
62	0	62	$2,000

(Continues)

Table 2-1 (Continued)

63	0	63	$2,000
64	0	64	$2,000
65	0	65	$2,000

PRINCIPLE 2: STRIVE FOR CONSISTENCY

Allied with having a long-term view is having an orientation geared toward investment consistency. In investing, hitting a lot of singles over many years is better than hitting a few home runs and occasionally striking out. Table 2-2 illustrates the power of consistency. As the table shows, the consistent but unspectacular results provide a greater ending balance over the five year period than the dramatic but wider swinging performance.

Table 2-2 Consistent versus Variable Returns

	Year 1	Year 2	Year 3	Year 4	Year 5
Investor A	+11%	+11%	+11%	+11%	+11%
Investor B	+20%	-50%	+50%	+30%	+15%

Total Return for:	Investor A	Investor B
Each Dollar Invested:	$1.68	$1.35

PRINCIPLE 3: DIVERSIFY YOUR INVESTMENTS

The best way for the individual investor to reduce risk is to diversify across different types of investments. The old folk saying of not putting all your eggs in one basket is a common way of expressing this principle. A "what if" scenario can best illustrate the advantages of diversification. If you have an even 50-50 percent split of investment dollars between stocks and a money market fund, and if the stock market should suddenly drop by a sickening 30 percent, your total investment accumulations would only be reduced by 15 percent. Moreover, if you had one-third of your funds in stocks, one-third in a money market fund and one-third in bonds at the time of the stock market sell-off, then the total reduction in accumulated value of your account would be only about 10 percent, hardly enough of a decline to cause major emotional trauma. By making use of several different investment vehicles, overall loss is minimized should a disaster befall any one of them.

Besides diversifying by investment vehicle (for example, stocks, bonds, cash equivalents, precious metals and real estate), you should diversify your investments by country as well. While the world's economies are linked, various countries experience different cycles of growth and very different patterns of investment performance. In Chapters Four, Five, and Six we aid in this diversification effort through a discussion of three regions of the globe where exceptional investment opportunities exist.

Not only is it important to diversify by investment vehicle and region of the world, but you should also diversify by investment strategy. There are many ways to manage your investment money. By using more than one strategy simultaneously, you reduce the risk of loss from problems associated with any one of them. Strategies that work well over one period of time may fall flat during other times. This is a sobering part of the reality that makes investing difficult. The wise investor understands that there is no best way to invest but there are many good ways. Diversifying among more than one strategy improves the odds that something will be "working" for you all the time. Chapters Seven through Eleven provide an array of strategies from which you can choose.

PRINCIPLE 4: MAKE INCREMENTAL CHANGES IN YOUR INVESTMENTS

If you are fortunate enough to have a working crystal ball, we recommend moving all of your investment money when the ball gives its advice to make a change. If, for example, you knew for certain that Japanese stocks would double in value next year, then you would be foolish not to put all of your money into Japanese stocks. You also might want to borrow money and even sell your house to raise money to invest in these stocks.

For those of us who must make financial decisions without the benefit of a perfect source of information, an all-or-nothing approach makes little sense. A realistic model of the financial markets and of the world in general should make use of probabilities. An incremental approach to buying and selling requires money to be moved in portions rather than all at once. This method allows you to adjust your investment exposure in approximate proportion with the degree of certainty and uncertainty you have toward the future direction of investment prices.

PRINCIPLE 5: KEEP IT SIMPLE

Most investors have years ahead of them for building an investment portfolio, many have decades. Unless your financial management system is straightforward, it will sooner or later be neglected. The methods we discuss in this book are simple in their understanding and execution so they can be easily maintained over the years. Whatever investment plan you choose for yourself, be sure that you understand it fully so that you can maintain it over the long-term.

PRINCIPLE 6: CHOOSE THE RIGHT INVESTMENT VEHICLES

There are many ways that you can invest internationally. It is important that you choose the investment vehicle or vehicles that support your goals and risk tolerance. To aid you in this endeavor, we'll review the options that you have.

U.S. Multinational Companies

One approach to investing internationally that many investors feel comfortable with is the purchase of shares of U.S. multinational companies. These shares are traded on U.S. exchanges, have familiar names, and pay out dividends in dollars like any other U.S.

company. What makes them different is the extent of their foreign operations. Investment in these global organizations allow you to participate in the economic growth of foreign economies while keeping your money at home.

As an example, International Business Machines (IBM) has over 50 percent of its assets in foreign countries and over 60 percent of its profits come from outside the U.S. Although its world headquarters is in the United States, it could be argued that it is more a "foreign-operations" company than a "U.S. operations" company. Coca-Cola is another prominent example, with nearly 60 percent of revenues coming from foreign sources. As more countries reduce their trade barriers, we can expect this 60 percent figure to rise even further.

Table 2-3 provides a list of major U.S. multinationals that obtain a substantial portion of their revenues from foreign sales, thereby having the potential to benefit from global economic growth.

Table 2-3 Large U.S. Multinational Corporations

CHEMICALS
   American Cyanamid
   Avery International
   Cabot Corp.
   Dow Chemical
   Du Pont
   W.R. Grace
   Great Lakes Chemical
   International Flavors and Fragrances
   Monsanto
   Morton International
   Rohm and Haas

ELECTRONICS
   Advanced Micro Devices
   AMP Inc.
   Applied Magnetics
   Bausch & Lomb
   Beckman Instruments
   Foxboro Co.
   Intel

(Continues)

Table 2-3 (Continued)

Measurex
Perkin-Elmer
Sprague Technologies
Tecktronics

ENERGY RELATED
Amoco
Atlantic Richfield
Chevron
Exxon
Haliburton
Mobil Corp.
Phillips Petroleum
Texaco
Unocal

FINANCIAL
American Express
Citicorp
Chase Manhattan
BankAmerica
Bank of Boston
Bankers Trust New York
JP Morgan & Co.
Salomon
Security Pacific

FOOD AND TOBACCO
American Brands
Coca-Cola
CPC International
H.J. Heinz
Kellogg
McDonald's
PepsiCo
Philip Morris
Quaker Oats
Sara Lee
Wm. Wrigley

MACHINERY
Baker Hughes

(Continues)

Table 2-3 (Continued)

Dresser Industries
  Foster Wheeler
  Ingersoll-Rand
  Interlake Corp.

MANUFACTURING
  Aluminum Company of America
  Black and Decker
  Eastman Kodak
  Minnesota Mining and Manufacturing
  United Technologies
  Westinghouse Electric

OFFICE EQUIPMENT
  Amdahl Corp.
  Apple Computer
  Cray Research
  Digital Equipment
  GTE
  Hewlett-Packard
  IBM
  Microsoft Corp.
  Motorola
  NCR Corp.
  Tandem Computer
  Texas Instruments
  Unisys Corp.
  Xerox

RETAILING AND PERSONAL PRODUCTS
  Avon Products
  Colgate-Palmolive
  Gillette
  K mart
  Proctor and Gamble
  Sears, Roebuck
  Woolworth

TRANSPORTATION-RELATED
  Boeing
  Chrysler
  Cummins Engine

(Continues)

Table 2-3 (Continued)

Ford Motor Co.
General Motors
Goodyear Tire and Rubber

The Value Line Investment Survey (711 Third Avenue, New York, NY 10017) is a good source for information on percentage of revenues that come from foreign operations or sales to foreign countries. Other good sources of information include annual reports and the Dow Jones News Retrieval Service (see the discussion of information sources later in this chapter for additional information on this service).

U.S. multinational companies will face many opportunities as the world economy expands. As European integration moves forward, companies with recognized brand names and an established distribution system will have an edge over the competition. As the rigid Communist systems are replaced with free-market economies, the resources of the multinationals will allow them to obtain a significant presence in these emerging markets. Moreover, the trend throughout the world toward the removal of trade and investment barriers creates further opportunities for expanding markets.

While multinationals offer an excellent vehicle for global investment diversification, special factors must be considered. These companies are especially sensitive to changes in exchange rates. When the U.S. dollar weakens, U.S. exports become less expensive from the viewpoint of the importing nation, thereby attracting buyers and boosting revenues. Moreover, the foreign currency sales and earnings of overseas affiliates are converted into more dollars, further increasing the multinationals' profits. The opposite effect occurs when the dollar strengthens; sales can be expected to drop, and foreign conversion back into U.S. dollars becomes unfavorable.

Purchasing multinationals as an international investment play tends to result in a shotgun rather than a rifle approach to investing. It is difficult to find a multinational that restricts its investments to a single country, so your investment dollars are diversi-fied—perhaps in some places you would rather not see them.

American Depositary Receipts (ADR's)

Another alternative for foreign investing is to purchase shares of foreign companies themselves. American investors who wish to buy shares of these companies but do not want the hassle of buying them directly on a foreign exchange, should look at the opportuni-ties of American Depositary Receipts. ADR's are receipts for stocks of specific foreign companies issued by American banks and trust companies. A U.S. or foreign correspondent bank holds the actual stock in a custodial account, receives dividends and converts them to dollars, pays any foreign taxes, and passes the amounts on to the investor. By trading in these investment vehicles you avoid the de-lays of trade settlement (which can take weeks in some countries), the trouble of safeguarding foreign stock certificates, and you elimi-nate the trouble of making currency exchanges. Furthermore, ADR's avoid the problem of foreign *and* domestic tax consequences that direct investments often carry.

The market value of an ADR reflects the current rate of exchange between the U.S. and a foreign country. This can of course work to either the benefit or the detriment of the investor. ADR's are traded on the New York Stock Exchange, the American Stock Exchange, NASDAQ, and on the over-the-counter pink sheets. While there are nearly 900 ADR's available, most are large capitalization issues that represent just a very small fraction of all foreign corporations in existence. It is also important to realize that an ADR may not repre-sent a single share of foreign stock. An ADR on a German stock may represent one-fifth of a share, and on a Japanese stock it may represent ten or more shares. This method of ADR pricing provides a single ADR with a dollar value similar to that of a U.S. stock. Table 2.4 provides a listing of some major ADR's. You will see that many of them are household names.

Mutual Funds

Mutual funds allow you to invest internationally without having to select individual securities. All transactions take place in conjunction with U.S. investment companies and are in U.S. dollars. They provide professional management at low cost and offer a diversified group of securities that an individual investor with a modest international portfolio would find impossible to match. Moreover, recordkeeping is easy to maintain and liquidity allows for rapid purchase and sale.

Table 2.4 Selected Major Foreign Stocks as ADR's

Country/Company	Where Traded
AUSTRALIA	
Broken Hill Properties	(NYSE)
National Australia	(NYSE)
News Corp.	(NYSE)
Pacific Dunlop	(NASDAQ)
AUSTRIA	
Veitscher Magnesit	(OTC)
BELGIUM	
Petrofina SA	(OTC)
BERMUDA	
ADT Ltd.	(NASDAQ)
Jardine Matheson	(OTC)
FINLAND	
Nokia	(OTC)
FRANCE	
BSN	(OTC)
Elf Aquitaine Group	(OTC)
LVMH	(NASDAQ)
L'Oreal	(OTC)
Peugeot	(OTC)
GERMANY	
BASF	(OTC)
Bayer	(OTC)
Continental	(OTC)
Daimler-Benz	(OTC)

(Continues)

Table 2-4 (Continued)

Deutsche Bank	(OTC)
Dresdner Bank	(NASDAQ)
Hoechse	(OTC)
Siemens	(OTC)
Thyssen	(OTC)
Volkswagen	(OTC)
HONG KONG	
Cathay Pacific	(OTC)
Cheung Kong	(OTC)
China Light and Power	(OTC)
Hong Kong and Shanghai Bank	(OTC)
Hutchison	(OTC)
Swire Pacific	(OTC)
ITALY	
Fiat	(NYSE)
Montedison	(NYSE)
STET	(OTC)
JAPAN	
Canon	(NASDAQ)
Fuji Heavy Industries	(OTC)
Fuji Photo	(NASDAQ)
Hitachi	(NYSE)
Honda	(NYSE)
Komatsu	(OTC)
Kyocera	(NYSE)
Matsushita	(NYSE)
Mitsubishi	(OTC)
Nintendo	(OTC)
Nissan	(OTC)
Pioneer	(NYSE)
Sony	(NYSE)
Tokio Marine and Fire	(NASDAQ)
Toyota	(NASDAQ)
MALAYSIA	
Sime Darby	(OTC)
MEXICO	
Cifra	(OTC)

(Continues)

Table 2-4 (Continued)

Grupo Sidek	(NASDAQ)
Ponderosa Industrial	(NASDAQ)
Telefonos de Mexico	(NASDAQ)
NETHERLANDS	
AEGON NV	(NASDAQ)
Akzo Group	(NASDAQ)
Heinekin	(OTC)
Philips	(NYSE)
Royal Dutch Petroleum	(NYSE)
Unilever	(NYSE)
NEW ZEALAND	
Brierley Investments	(OTC)
Fletcher Challenge	(OTC)
NORWAY	
Hafslund Nycomed	(OTC)
Norsk Data	(NASDAQ)
Norsk Hydro	(NYSE)
SINGAPORE	
Development Bank	(OTC)
Keppel	(OTC)
Neptune Orient Lines	(OTC)
SOUTH AFRICA	
Buffelsfontein Gold	(NASDAQ)
DeBeers	(NASDAQ)
Kloof Gold	(OTC)
SWEDEN	
ASEA	(NASDAQ)
SKF Group	(NASDAQ)
Volvo	(NASDAQ)
UNITED KINGDOM	
Attwoods	(NASDAQ)
Barclays	(NYSE)
Beazer	(NYSE)
British Airways	(NYSE)

(Continues)

Table 2-4 (Continued)

British Gas	(NYSE)
British Petroleum	(NYSE)
British Steel	(NYSE)
British Telecom	(NYSE)
B.A.T. Industries	(ASE)
Cable and Wireless	(NYSE)
Cadbury Schweppes	(NASDAQ)
Glaxo Holding	(NYSE)
Grand Metropolitan	(OTC)
Hanson	(NYSE)
Imperial Chemical	(NYSE)
Manpower	(NYSE)
National Westminster	(NYSE)
Racal Telecom	(NYSE)
Reuters	(NASDAQ)
SmithKline Beecham	(NYSE)
Wellcome	(OTC)

There are two types of mutual funds; open-end and closed-end. An open-end mutual fund issues new shares as investments are made and redeems shares when investors sell. The share price of the fund represents the market value of the securities that the fund holds. Open-end funds can be further divided into load funds and no-load funds. Load funds charge a sales commission when shares are purchased, sold, or the fee is assessed on an annual basis. No-load funds do not charge a sales commission. The potential disadvantage with no-load funds is that there are no sales people available to help you decide which fund to buy. With these funds it is necessary for you to do your own research and buy them directly from the investment company offering them. Table 2-5 provides a listing of no-load open-ended mutual funds involved in international investments. In general, "global" funds invest in U.S. securities markets as well as those in other countries while "international" funds invest only in securities markets outside the United States.

Considerable academic research has been done comparing the performance of load and no-load mutual funds. These studies have found that load funds do not perform better than no-load funds. In fact, they actually perform less well, on aggregate, by the amount of the sales fee. This makes sense, as the sales load is a commission paid to salesmen, not a fee to the managers of the fund. The bottom line for "do-it-yourself" investors is to look first in Table 2-5 for an international fund. If the type of fund that you want is not available as a no-load fund, *then* look to the load funds. Table 2-6 provides a listing of the load (sales-commission) funds.

Table 2-5 Global and International No-Load Mutual Funds: Open-Ended

Equity (Stock) Funds
    Financial Strategic Portfolio—European (800) 525-8085
    Financial Strategic Portfolio—Pacific Basin
    IAI International (612) 371-2884
    International Equity Trust (800) 845-8406
    IVY International (800) 235-3322
    Nomura Pacific Basin (800) 833-0018
    T. Rowe International Stock (800) 638-5660
    Scudder Global (800) 225-2470
    Scudder International (800) 225-2470
    Scudder Japan (800) 225-2470
    Transatlantic Growth (800) 237-4218
    Vanguard Trustees' Commingled-International
      Portfolio (800) 662-7447
    Vanguard World—International (800) 662-7447
    USAA International (800) 531-8000

Bond Funds
    Fidelity Global Bond (800) 544-6666
    T. Rowe Price International Bond (800) 638-5660
    Transatlantic Income (800) 237-4218

Money Market Funds
    Dreyfus World-Wide Dollar (800) 645-6561

(Continues)

Table 2-5 (Continued)

Gold Funds
   Financial Strategic Portfolio—Gold (800) 525-8085
   Lexington Goldfund (800) 526-0056
   USAA Gold (800) 531-8000
   US Gold Shares (800) 873-8637
   US New Prospector (800) 873-8637
   Vanguard Gold and Precious Metals (800) 662-7447

Table 2-6 Global and International Load (Sales-Commission) Mutual Funds: Open-Ended

Fund	Telephone	Load
Equity (Stock) Funds		
Alliance Global-Canadian	(800) 523-5695	5.50%
Alliance International	(800) 523-5695	5.50%
Capstone Int. European Plus	(800) 262-6631	4.75%
Dean Witter World Wide	(800) 869-3863	5.00%
Dreyfus Strategic World	(800) 782-6620	3.00%
Enterprise International Gr.	(800) 432-4320	4.75%
Europacific Growth	(800) 421-0180	5.75%
European Emerging Companies	(800) 523-2578	4.50%
Fenimore International Equity	(800) 223-4522	5.00%
Fidelity Canada	(800) 544-8888	3.00%
Fidelity Europe	(800) 544-8888	3.00%
Fidelity Int. Growth & Inc.	(800) 544-8888	2.00%
Fidelity Overseas Fund	(800) 544-8888	3.00%
Fidelity Pacific Basin	(800) 544-8888	3.00%
First Investor's Global	(800) 423-4026	6.90%
Flag Investors Int. Trust	(800) 767-3524	4.50%
Freedom Inv.II Global	(800) 225-6258	5.00%
FT International	(800) 356-2805	4.50%
GAM Europe	(800) 356-5740	5.00%
GAM Global	(800) 356-5740	5.00%

(Continues)

Table 2-6 (Continued)

GAM International	(800) 356-5740	5.00%
GAM Pacific Basin	(800) 356-5740	5.00%
GT Global-Europe	(800) 824-1580	4.75%
GT Global-International	(800) 824-1580	4.75%
GT Global-Japan	(800) 824-1580	4.75%
GT Global-Pacific	(800) 824-1580	4.75%
GT Global-Worldwide	(800) 824-1580	4.75%
John Hancock Global Trust	(800) 225-5291	4.50%
John Hancock World-Pac. Basin.	(800) 225-5291	4.50%
IDS International Fund	(800) 328-8300	5.00%
IDS Strategy-Pan Pacific Gr.	(800) 328-8300	5.00%
Kemper International	(800) 621-1148	5.75%
Keystone International	(800) 343-2898	4.00%
Lexington Global Fund	(800) 526-0056	5.00%
Lord Abbett Global-Equity	(800) 426-1130	6.75%
Mackenzie Canada Fund	(800) 456-5111	5.00%
Mainstay Global (M-S)	(800) 522-4202	5.00%
Merrill Lynch Eurofund	(800) 637-3863	6.50%
Merrill Lynch Global Alloc.	(800) 637-3863	6.50%
Merrill Lynch Global Convert.	(800) 637-3863	4.00%
Merrill Lynch Int. Holdings	(800) 637-3863	6.50%
Merrill Lynch Pacific Fund	(800) 637-3863	6.50%
MFS Lifetime Global Eq. Trust	(800) 225-2606	6.00%
Oppenheimer Global Bio-tech.	(800) 525-7048	6.75%
Oppenheimer Global Fund	(800) 525-7048	8.50%
Paine Webber Classic Atlas	(800) 544-9300	4.50%
Paine Webber Classic World	(800) 544-9300	4.50%
Princor World Fund	(800) 247-4123	5.00%
Provident Mutual World	(800) 441-9490	6.00%
Pru-Bache Global Fund	(800) 225-1852	5.25%
Pru-Bache Global Genesis	(800) 225-1852	5.25%
Pru-Bache Global Nat. Resources	(800) 225-1852	5.25%
Putnam International Equities	(800) 225-1581	5.75%
Rodney Square International Eq.	(800) 225-5084	5.75%
Shearson LH Equity-Int.	(212) 528-2744	5.00%

(Continues)

Table 2-6 (Continued)

Shearson LH Global Opport.	(212) 528-2744	5.00%
Shearson LH Inv. Global Equity	(212) 528-2744	5.00%
Templeton Foreign Fund	(800) 237-0738	8.50%
Templeton Global Fund	(800) 237-0738	8.50%
Templeton Growth Fund	(800) 237-0738	8.50%
Thomson McKinnon Global	(800) 628-1237	5.00%
Transamerica Spec. Global Gr.	(800) 999-3863	6.00%
Tyndall-Newport Far East	(800) 527-9500	5.00%
Tyndall-Newport Tiger	(800) 527-9500	5.00%
United International Growth	(800) 366-5465	8.50%
UST Master Funds-Int	(800) 233-1136	4.50%
Van Eck International Inv.	(800) 221-2220	8.50%
Van Eck World Trends Fund	(800) 221-2220	5.75%
Warburg International Fund	(212) 363-3300	4.50%

Bond Funds
Capital World Bond Fund	(800) 421-0180	4.75%
Dean Witter Worldwide Income	(800) 869-3863	5.00%
Freedom Inv. II Global Income	(800) 225-6258	3.00%
GT Investment-Global Bond	(800) 824-1580	4.75%
Mass Financial Intl-Bond	(800) 225-2606	4.75%
Merrill Lynch Retire Global Bond	(800) 637-3863	4.00%
Paine Webber Mstr Global Income	(800) 544-9300	5.00%
Putnam Global Governmantal	(800) 225-1581	4.75%
Shearson LH Income-Global Bond	(212) 528-2744	5.00%
Van Eck World Income Fund	(212) 221-2220	4.75%

Precious Metals Funds
Enterprise Group Precious Metals	(800) 432-4320	4.75%
Franklin Gold Fund	(800) 342-5236	4.00%
IDS Precious Metals Fund	(800) 328-8300	5.00%
Keystone Precious Metals Fund	(800) 343-2898	4.00%
MFS Lifetime Gold & Prec. Metals	(800) 225-2606	6.00%
Shearson LH Precious Metals	(212) 528-2744	5.00%

Foreign Currency Funds
Fidelity Deutschemark L.P.	(800) 544-8888	0.40%

(Continues)

Table 2-6 (Continued)

Fidelity Sterling L.P.	(800) 544-8888	0.40%
Fidelity Yen L.P.	(800) 544-8888	0.40%

Note: Sales Charges (loads) shown represent maximum charges based on assessments made when shares are purchased and sold. Actual charges may be less that those specified based on the amount of time that the shares are held or the dollar amount of shares purchased. Loads may also have changed (higher or lower) by the time you purchase this book. Do not assume the loads shown are correct. For current charges, obtain and read the fund's most recent prospectus.

The other type of mutual fund is the closed-end fund. This classification of fund trades on an exchange like ordinary shares of stock. Because it is traded, its current price may or may not equal its net asset value. It may sell at a premium or a discount to its net asset value depending on supply-demand conditions. To buy or sell these funds you simply call your stockbroker just like you would for a U.S. stock. Of course, a sales commission will be charged based on the number of shares transacted. Table 2-7 provides a listing of available international closed-end mutual funds on American exchanges.

Closed-end funds are often the only way to buy a mutual fund of a single country. Despite their popularity as an international investing vehicle, there are problems. It is often difficult to obtain current information on the composition of a fund, and during a market decline they may trade at a deep discount to their net asset value. This volatility makes them more of a speculative international investment than open-end funds that always sell at their net asset value. If you are a risk averse investor, it is best to look to other international investment vehicles. For the aggressive investor, they provide an easy-to-use vehicle to participate in the securities markets of individual countries. Besides purchasing mutual funds on U.S. exchanges, it is also possible to buy international mutual funds

Table 2-7 Closed-End International Mutual Funds

Fund	Where Traded
Asia Pacific Fund	NYSE
Austria Fund	NYSE
Brazil Fund	NYSE
Chile Fund	NYSE
Cypress Fund	AMEX
Emerging Germany Fund	NYSE
Emerging Mexico Fund	NYSE
Europe Fund	NYSE
European Warrant Fund	NYSE
First Australian Fund	AMEX
First Philippine Fund	NYSE
First Iberian Fund	AMEX
France Growth Fund	NYSE
Future Germany Fund	NYSE
G.T. Greater Europe Fund	NYSE
Germany Fund	NYSE
Growth Fund of Spain	NYSE
India Fund	NYSE
Indonesia Fund (The)	NYSE
Italy Fund	NYSE
Irish Investment Fund	NYSE
Jakarta Growth Fund	NYSE
Japan OTC Equity Fund	NYSE
Korea Fund	NYSE
Latin American Investment Fund	NYSE
Malaysia Fund	NYSE
Mexico Equity and Income Fund	NYSE
Mexico Fund	NYSE
New Germany Fund	NYSE
Pacific European Growth	AMEX
Portugal Fund	NYSE
ROC Taiwan Fund	NYSE

(Continues)

Table 2-7 (Continued)

Scudder New Asia Fund	NYSE
Scudder New Europe Fund	NYSE
Singapore Fund	NYSE
Spain Fund	NYSE
Swiss Helvetia Fund	NYSE
Taiwan Fund	NYSE
Templeton Global Income Fund	NYSE
Templeton Global Government Fund	NYSE
Templeton Global Utility Fund	AMEX
Thai Capital Fund	NYSE
Thai Fund	NYSE
Turkish Investment Fund	NYSE
United Kingdom Fund	NYSE
World Income Fund	AMEX
Worldwide Value Fund	NYSE

NYSE = New York Stock Exchange
AMEX = American Stock Exchange

through foreign banks. In Chapter Three we will discuss this avenue for foreign investment.

Foreign Company Shares on Foreign Markets

The most direct way to participate in international security ownership is through the purchase of shares of stock on a foreign exchange. One approach to buying foreign securities is to contact a major domestic broker such as Merrill Lynch or a money center bank such as Citicorp and have them handle the trading for you. While this method will work in most major international markets, in some countries the domestic broker may not be able to trade. In these cases it is necessary to contact a foreign bank or broker that is registered to trade on the exchange where your security trades.

Like the truck rental company that advertises an "Adventure in Moving," you are likely to experience an "Adventure in Transacting" if you choose to use the foreign bank or broker approach to security ownership. You may find problems with language differences, currency exchange, foreign taxes, settlement delays and account safety. Moreover, in some countries there are restrictions on foreign ownership of securities, making it difficult or even illegal to trade. During the great Taiwan bull market that ended in 1990, it was estimated that of the four million stock accounts in the country, about one million were surrogate accounts actually owned and controlled by foreigners or locals who wished to remain anonymous, so as to avoid foreign ownership restrictions or taxes. Most investors would like to avoid such unethical measures, but it is sometimes the only way to make a direct investment in a foreign market.

If you wish to invest directly, it will be important for you to understand foreign currency and the role it plays in owning foreign stocks. You must know where to find information on foreign currency values and how to calculate what another country's currency is worth in terms of U.S. dollars. Appendix A provides an example of exchange rate information and shows how conversions from dollars to a foreign currency, and conversely, from a foreign currency to dollars, can be made. It will be important for you to understand this process thoroughly before attempting to buy foreign shares directly.

Options/Futures

Another vehicle for foreign investment is the use of options or futures on foreign securities and market indexes. We think that for the vast majority of individual investors this approach carries too much risk. Options and futures are highly volatile and speculative financial instruments best left to the professional traders and risk-seeking speculators. If you want to follow this path anyway, the following books contain information useful for you, and should be used as a starting point for your long speculative journey: 1) *The Dow Jones-Irwin Guide to International Securities, Futures, and Options Markets* by William and Susan Nix (Dow Jones Irwin, 1988), 2) *The Dow Jones-Irwin Guide to Trading Systems* by Bruce Babcock, Jr. (Dow Jones-Irwin, 1989), and 3) *Trading Stock Index Options*, by Mikel T. Dodd (Probus Publishing, 1988).

Real Estate

Still another way to make an international investment is through real estate ownership. Real estate is an investment that gives great pleasure to many people—a pleasure that often goes far beyond that of holding stock certificates or looking at a quarterly statement from a mutual fund investment company. Finding a bargain in a foreign country that you can use during holidays and later sell or retire to on a full time basis is certainly appealing. Not only does this investment offer the potential for current enjoyment, but it also provides a hedge against long-term inflation and a declining dollar. Unfortunately, foreign real estate ownership is fraught with risks as well as carrying potential rewards. In Chapter 11 we discuss in detail this important international investment topic.

PRINCIPLE 7: CREATE YOUR OWN INTERNATIONAL INFORMATION SYSTEM

Obtaining timely global investment information will require you to make a greater effort than what is necessary to support your domestic investments. The creation of your own on-going international information system is the best way to insure that your portfolio will not suffer from informational neglect. Your information system should provide you with both general information on world economic events and specific information concerning markets and investment vehicles of special interest to you. Fortunately, there are many good information sources that are available for your use.

Periodicals

You can keep up on major international happenings and have a good overall feel for world financial events by reading major financial newspapers. Barron's weekly newspaper, with its International Trader section provides an excellent one-page capsule of international economic events around the world. A quick reading of this one page summary each week will allow you, over time, to know which economies look favorable and which look unfavorable for investment purposes. It is must reading for serious international investors.

The Barrons' section also provides index data on individual stock markets (including emerging markets) as well as giving an international stock market composite index. These indexes can be plotted on graph paper (or with your computer) each week as an indicator of how equities, on a world-wide basis, are faring.

Another good source of general information comes from the daily financial newspapers. The best of these is the *Financial Times* of London, whose only major drawback is its limited availability in the U.S. *The Wall Street Journal*, and *Investor's Daily* also have international coverage, although not as complete as the *Financial Times*.

Magazines are other sources, with *The Economist, Business Week, Forbes,* and *Fortune* representing good choices for sources of general international investment information. *Capital International Perspectives* (3 Place Des Bergues, 1201 Geneva, Switzerland) is a monthly publication that deals with international investments and also provides valuable information for the global investor.

In later chapters of this book you will learn of periodicals that address specific countries and world regions.

Newsletters

The advantage of newsletters is that they integrate and summarize information from many sources. Some newsletters provide general international information only while others make specific investment recommendations. Many newsletters are available for the international arena. The following review, although not comprehensive, should provide an idea of the types of newsletters available. Names and addresses of additional newsletters can be found among the advertisements in *Barron's, Investors Daily,* and from the *Select Information Exchange*, newsletter catalog, (244 West 54th Street 7th floor, New York, NY 10019).

The International Bank Credit Analyst (J. Anthony Boeckh, Editor-in Chief, BCA Publications, 3463 Peel Street, Montreal, Quebec, Canada H3A 1W7, $595 per year) is one of the most widely respected newsletters for the international investor. This monthly publication provides an analysis and forecast of interest rates, equity markets, gold and commodity prices, economic trends and currency movements for major countries. The forecasting approach is based on a continuous appraisal of money, credit and policy trends on a global basis.

Global Fund Timer (Greg Cook, Editor, P.O. Box 77330, Baton Rouge, LA 70879, $149 per year) is a monthly publication devoted to timing the purchase and sale of global mutual funds. The newsletter provides a global model portfolio that makes use of Fidelity mutual funds. For timing U.S. securities, an S&P 500 composite model is used that is made up of five different indicators. A consensus approach is used based on the number of indicators that are giving positive or negative readings. Separate timing systems are also provided for gold, international markets, bonds, and technology funds. A hotline, updated twice weekly is also available.

Pring Market Review (Martin J. Pring, Editor, P.O. Box 338, Washington Depot, CT 06794, $355 per year) is a monthly newsletter that summarizes the status of world financial markets with an emphasis on technical analysis. Besides the U.S. stock market, Germany, the U.K., Japan, Canada, Australia, France, Italy, Denmark, Singapore and Hong Kong are analyzed in detail using graphs and descriptive material. Besides the equity markets, this publication analyzes debt markets, currencies, precious metals and commodities.

Worldwide Investment News (J.F. Straw, Editor, 301 Plymouth Drive N.E., Dalton, GA, $90 per year) is a monthly publication that offers information on international business connections, mutual funds, trust services and other investment services.

Correspondents in twenty-three different countries report on significant events world-wide. The publication also reviews books on international business and answers subscriber's questions in a letters-to-the-editor column. The newsletter also contains an international resources directory which lists providers of services in international banking, business and investments. A "Business Opportunities" section provides classified advertisements for international business offerings.

Dessaur's Journal (Limmat Publications, Inc., P.O. Box 1718, Orleans, MA 02653, $195 per year) is a monthly publication that provides a global perspective on investing. Major markets are individually discussed, and a recommended global investment strategy is provided, listing individual securities and percentage of portfolio allocations. The performance of all recommended investments is tracked each month. John Dessaur's editorial column, "Profitable Perspectives," typically provides a unique and personal look at significant world events.

International Fund Monitor (Jon Woronoff, Publisher, P.O. Box 5754 Washington, D.C., $84 per year) is a monthly newsletter that provides to-the-point summaries of world markets, currencies, economics, political developments, and mutual funds. Moreover, each issue gives an in-depth look at three special topics that are of interest to the global investor.

Computer On-Line Services

The most comprehensive source of current information for the serious international investor is from on-line information systems. Of the services available, the best on-line service for this information is Dow-Jones News Retrieval. With a personal computer and modem, it is possible to access this information source 24 hours a day. (Dow Jones News Retrieval, P.O. Box 300, Princeton, NJ 08543-0300). Vast amounts of specific information is provided by this Dow Jones electronic service. Some of the major information sources include:

1. *Dow Jones International News (symbol //DJINS).* This service provides coverage of foreign exchange, money and capital markets, company and industry news, investment news and trends from major foreign exchanges, and country-by-country financial market round ups. Along with news and statistics, this service provides commentaries and analyses that explain the effects of international events on the markets and business world. Information is provided by Dow Jones' international newswire services, *The Wall Street Journal, The Wall Street Journal/Europe,* and *The Asian Wall Street Journal.* Specific subtopics within the international news database are shown in Table 2-8.

2. *Dow Jones News (symbol //DJNEWS).* This is another database that provides information of value to the international investor. This service contains news from the Dow Jones News Service (the Broadtape or the ticker) including the Canadian Dow Jones News Service as well as articles from *The Wall Street Journal* and *Barron's.*

Table 2-8 Dow Jones International News Subtopic Categories

All Current-Day News	International Stock Markets
Australia	Italy
Bahrain	Japan
Belgium	Netherlands
Britain	New Zealand
Denmark	News Calendar
Europe	Norway
Finland	Philippines
France	Portugal
Hong Kong	Saudi Arabia
"Hot" News	Singapore
International Bond Markets	South Africa
International Commodity News	South Korea
International Economic News	Spain
International Equity News	Sweden
International Foreign	Switzerland
Exchange News	Taiwan
International News Summary	United States
International Petroleum News	Germany
International Precious	
Metals News	

Some of the specific news codes of interest to the international investor that can be selected include: 1) Africa, 2) Major international banks, 3) Canada, 4) Europe, 5) Far East, 6) Foreign Exchange News, 7) Foreign news, 8) International Economic News, 9) International Foreign Exchange News, 10) Japan, 11) Latin America/South America, 12) Middle East, and 13) State Department News.

3. *The INVEST database (symbol //INVEST).* The database INVEST provides in-depth information on major foreign companies. The information comes from research reports written by both domestic and foreign investment specialists. Because of the diversity of providers, this information would be impossible for the individual in-

vestor to obtain on a timely basis, except through this service. A list
of providers is shown in Table 2-9.

4. *The KYODO database (symbol //KYODO).* This database has
news on Japanese markets, companies, products and technology, as
provided by Kyodo News International and published in *Japan Economic Daily.*

Table 2-9 Providers of Foreign Corporation Analysis Reports

Advest Inc.	Mabon, Nugent & Company
Algemene Bank Nederland	Market Guide, Inc.
Balis Zorn Gerard Inc.	McLeod Young Weir Limited
Banca Commerciale Italiana	Merrill Lynch Inc.
Bear, Sterns & Co.	Morgan Stanley & Co. Inc.
J.C. Bradford & Co.	Moseley Securities Corp.
Alex. Brown & Sons, Inc.	N. Y. Society of Sec. Analysts
Butcher & Singer, Inc.	Nomura Securities International
Cable, Howse & Ragen	Oppenheimer & Company, Inc.
Citicorp Scrimgeour Vickers	PaineWebber, Inc
Craig-Hallum, Inc.	Phillips & Drew
DAFSA	Piper Jaffray & Hopwood Inc.
Dain Bosworth, Inc.	Provident National Bank
Dean Witter Reynolds	Prudential-Bache Securities
degab Deutsche Gesallschaft	Rauscher Pierce Refsnes, Inc.
Dillon, Read & Co. Inc.	Richardson Greenshields
Donaldson, Lufkin & Jenrette	Roach Tilley Grice, Inc.
Eberstadt Fleming, Inc.	Salomon Brothers Inc.
A.G. Edwards & Sons	Sanyo Securities America
First Boston Corporation	Shearson Lehman Brothers, Inc.
Fitch Investors Service, Inc.	Smith Barney Harris Upham & Co.
Fox-Pitt, Kelton, Inc.	Stephens, Inc.
Hibbard Brown & Co., Inc.	Sutro & Co.
Interstate Securities Corp.	Tucker, Anthony & R.L. Day, Inc.
Janney Montgomery Scott	Union Bank of Switzerland
Kidder, Peabody & Co., Inc.	Van Kasper & Co.
Kredietbank	Wertheim Schroder & Co. Inc.
C.J. Lawrence, Morgan Grenfell	Yamaichi Research Institute

6. *The Canada database (symbol //CANADA)*. This database offers business and market news and financial and market information on 2200 public, private and Crown (government owned) Canadian companies. Company news and reports are provided by Info Globe, publishers of Canada's national newspaper, *The Globe and Mail*.

7. *The TEXT database (symbol //TEXT)*. This database is the most sophisticated of all the Dow Jones databases. It provides the ability to search through articles from over a hundred publications based on multiple search terms connected by logical connectors such as AND, NOT, OR, SAME. For example, let's say you are interested in finding all articles published in *The Wall Street Journal* that discuss the Yen and American Honda car prices. By entering the words "American Honda" and "Yen," articles published in *The Wall Street Journal* since January, 1984 are searched to find all articles that contain these two words. You can display the headline and first page of each article, or you can select the full text of any of the articles.

Besides the Dow Jones News/Retrieval service, there are other electronic database services that have information for the individual investor. Although none provide as comprehensive a source of global information as the Dow Jones service, they are still worth considering as they may meet your requirements at (possibly) lower cost. A list of major global services is provided in Table 2-10. A comprehensive list of electronic domestic and global information services can be found in the annual, *The Individual Investor's Guide to Computerized Investing* (American Association of Individual Investors, 625 North Michigan Avenue, Chicago, IL 60611).

Table 2-10   Major Global Electronic Information Services

Automated Investments
Proquote
3284 Yonge Street, Suite 401
Toronto, Canada M4N 3M7

Compuserve
5000 Arlington Centre Boulevard
Columbus, OH 43220

Comstock
670 White Plains Road
Scarsdale, NY 10583

Disclosure, Inc.
Compact D/Canada, Compact D/Europe
5161 River Road
Bethesda, MD 20816

IDD Information Services
International Tradeline
150 Broadway
New York, NY 10038

Marketbase, Inc.
P.O. Box 826
New York, NY 10024-0826

Prodigy Services Company
445 Hamilton Avenue
White Plains, NY 10601

Public Brand Software
Business Cycle Indicators
P.O. Box 51315
Indianapolis, IN 46251

Warner Computer Systems
One University Plaza
Hackensack, NJ 07601

REFERENCES

Colby, Robert and Meyers, Thomas, *The Encyclopedia of Technical Market Indicators* (Homewood, IL: Dow Jones-Irwin, 1988).

Corney, William, *Dynamic Stock Market Analysis* (Homewood, IL: Dow Jones-Irwin, 1986).

Dow Jones News Retrieval Users Guide (Princeton, NJ: Dow Jones & Company, 1990).

Hirsch, Yale, *Don't Sell Stock on Monday* (New York, NY: Facts on File Publications, 1986).

Perritt, Gerald W., *The Mutual Fund Encyclopedia* (Chicago, IL: Dearborn Financial Publishing, 1990).

The Individual Investor's Guide to Computerized Investing (Chicago, IL: The American Association of Individual Investors, 8th Edition, 1991).

The Individual Investors Guide to No-Load Mutual Funds (Chicago, IL: The American Association of Individual Investors, International Publishing Corporation, 1990).

Smyth, David, *The Worldly Wise Investor*, (New York, NY: Franklin Watts, 1988).

Stoken, Richard A. *Strategic Investment Timing* (New York, NY: Macmillian, 1984).

Walden, Gene, *The 100 Best Stocks to Own in the World* (Chicago, IL: Dearborn Financial Publishing, 1990).

Warfield, Gerald, *How to Buy Foreign Stocks and Bonds* (New York, NY: Harper & Row, Publishers, 1985).

World Chamber of Commerce Directory, 1990, P.O. Box 1029, Loveland, CO 80539.

Zweig, Martin, *Martin Zweig's Winning with New IRS's*, Warner Books, 1987.

CHAPTER 3

Overseas Bank Accounts and Currencies

The increasing mobility of the modern world means that many individuals today will want to have a bank account in a foreign country (perhaps more than one). It is certainly very possible to have a globally oriented investment portfolio without an overseas bank account. Such accounts provide specific advantages, however, and there are reasons other than investing for opening an overseas account.

USING AN OVERSEAS ACCOUNT

Individuals have a variety of motivations for using an overseas bank account. Some relate directly to their business and investment activities. Others do not. We will consider several of the reasons for opening and using such an account.

Travel

One very common reason for establishing a bank account in a foreign country is because the individual travels there regularly. Some people vacation on the Mexican coast every summer or ski in Switzerland every winter. Many who travel for business reasons find themselves in the same foreign countries on a regular basis because that is where their businesses have offices, factories or marketing outlets.

It makes sense for such people to maintain a bank account in the countries to which their travels frequently take them. An account makes it convenient to pay bills locally. Also, maintaining an account in the local currency protects the individual from having to worry about currency fluctuations. The frequent traveler to Germany may constantly worry about the changing value of the dollar in relation to the deutschemark, but if an account is maintained in a German bank in the local currency, the money will be there to spend when needed, and its relationship to the dollar at any given time will be much less important.

Business

An individual or corporation doing business in a foreign country will nearly always need to have a bank account there. In addition to providing access to funds, the account will establish a local banking relationship which can be helpful in many ways. The local bank may become a source of credit if the businessman needs to borrow. It can facilitate the transfer of funds from one country to another. Just as at home, a good banking relationship in a foreign country can make the process of doing business much easier.

Retirement Plans

Some people may want to have an account in the location where they eventually plan to retire. More and more retirees are locating in a nation other than where they spent their working years. Many residents of the United States and Canada are moving to Mexico. The southern coast of Spain is a favorite retirement location for former residents of England and northern Europe.

A bank account can provide retirees many of the same advantages it provides for men and women in business. It establishes a local contact. It can be used when the individual travels to the area in the years prior to retirement. It makes it easier to transfer funds from home to the future retirement area, and it may provide a source of credit if the individual needs to borrow funds in that area after moving there.

Investment Services

The world-view investor with a relatively large portfolio may want to have one or more overseas accounts to facilitate investment transactions. An investor can open and use a foreign bank account for investment purposes even if he or she never plans to travel abroad. It is important to understand that foreign banks perform many functions which would be performed by brokerage houses or investment companies in the United States. Therefore, a relationship with a bank in a foreign country will provide access that one would have to go to several different financial institutions to obtain. A detailed discussion of the services available from foreign banks is provided later in this chapter.

Diversification

There is no investment principle more important than diversification, or asset allocation as it is sometimes called. A well planned balanced portfolio will include several different types of investments, including perhaps common stocks, corporate bonds, government bonds, real estate, precious metals and cash. Now that we live in a global economy it is equally important that we deliberately diversify on a worldwide basis. It would have made no sense in the past for an individual to have limited his or her investments to one or two states. It makes no sense today to limit them to one or two countries.

A relationship with a foreign bank provides access to investment information and services in that area. A bank in London or Geneva, for example, can be helpful in investing that portion of a portfolio which an individual wants to devote to European investments. Likewise, a bank in Hong Kong or Singapore should have special competence in investing funds in the Asian region. Today there are many international banks in places such as New York, Zurich or Hong Kong which will claim to have investment competence throughout the world. Common sense, however, suggests that banking officials or investment managers will tend to know their own area of the world best. As we discuss below, only investors with large portfolios will find it worthwhile to have multiple overseas accounts. The average investor may be better off to have just one overseas account with a bank in the area where that investor has a special interest.

World View

Some investors will have very personal reasons for wanting to have a foreign bank account. We refer to that as the investor's "world view." For example, in the days before the Cold War cooled off, many people feared that the United States would succumb to communistic or socialistic influences, and they wanted to keep a portion of their funds in a safe foreign location. When the price of oil increased sharply in the 1970's, many rulers of the oil rich countries of the Middle East found themselves with large amounts of cash. Because they viewed places such as Switzerland as providing a high degree of political and economic stability, they moved much of their wealth there. There are always rumors that certain dictators or political leaders in volatile countries around the world have secret bank accounts in Switzerland or elsewhere. Of course, this is an example of diversification and the search for financial privacy (discussed below) as well as world view.

The dramatic growth of Japan, Korea and other Asian economies has convinced some investors that Asia offers the best investment opportunities for the future. Other investors, looking at the political changes in eastern Europe and the economic unification of western Europe in 1992, believe that Europe is the place for the wise investor to be. These are examples of an investor's world view. Note the relationship of one's world view to the principle of diversification. Even though you may believe that Asia is the great investment opportunity for the next decade, it is never possible to be sure. Therefore, it is always important to maintain a prudent diversification in a portfolio.

Financial Privacy

There is no doubt that for many individuals a foreign bank account represents privacy, or financial confidentiality. It is equally true that bank accounts in the United States provide just the opposite. Federal legislation in the United States requires banks to report large transfers of funds and provides the Internal Revenue Service and other federal agencies access to information about individual bank accounts in certain cases.

Many people who have no intention of doing anything illegal simply believe that their financial status is no one else's business, and they use a foreign bank account to help protect that privacy. Financial privacy has a noble history. During the 1930's Nazi officials attempted to force Swiss banks to tell them whether Jewish residents of Germany had accounts there. The Swiss banks held firm, often in the face of great political and economic pressure, and by so doing they helped protect the financial privacy of many individuals. That was the beginning of the outstanding reputation of Swiss banks for the protection of financial privacy. More recently a number of international problems, including the use of overseas banks to hide money made in the illegal drug business, has caused many to question the practice of those nations which provide financial privacy. The current problems of using a foreign account to achieve financial privacy is explained in more detail below, in the discussion of bank services.

OVERSEAS BANK SERVICES

Most large overseas banks provide a wider range of services than American banks. This is partly the result of regulatory restrictions placed on banks in the United States, but it is also the result of tradition in many countries where businesses and investors have long looked to banking institutions for a comprehensive set of financial services. We will review here the most common services available from overseas banks.

Checking and Interest Bearing Accounts

Overseas banks provide the traditional services of *checking accounts* and *interest bearing accounts*. A checking account can serve the usual purposes of such an account. It enables the investor to pay bills and do business with funds drawn on a local bank. Either type of account can also serve as a place to "park money" until a decision is made as to the best place to invest it. Caution should be exercised, however, to check the restrictions which may apply to foreign accounts, especially interest bearing accounts. There may be limits as to when and how often funds may be transferred out of such accounts.

Unless an investor just wants to have money in a foreign bank for other reasons, the interest bearing account, what we would commonly call a savings account, may be of only limited value as an investment vehicle. There is a "catch-22" involved with such accounts. On the one hand, banks in countries with a strong currency, such as Switzerland, usually pay a relatively low interest rate on these accounts. In contrast, banks in countries with weaker currencies, such as Australia, will pay much higher interest rates, but the investor faces the risk of losing part of his or her principal if the value of that currency falls against other world currencies. A deposit in an account in such a country is really more of a speculation in currency fluctuation than it is a low-risk interest bearing investment. The best use of these accounts is as a vehicle for transacting business or providing funds for other investments rather than being attractive investment instruments themselves.

Multi-Currency Accounts

One particular type of checking account which may be very useful to some individuals is the *multi-currency account*. Some foreign banks will allow the depositor to indicate, when writing checks, which of several currencies to use in paying the check. This is especially useful in an area like Europe, where there are many countries each with their own currency. This gives the depositor the ability to pay bills in the local currency of the country in which he is traveling. Alternatively, it provides an opportunity to pay bills in whichever is the strongest currency at the moment; this is a case where the individual can choose the currency which gives literally "the most bang for the buck."

Investment Management

For the larger investor a very important function of overseas banks is the provision of *investment management services*. As noted above, foreign banks often provide the services that a brokerage house or investment company might provide in the United States. These banks will provide personalized management of funds, purchasing local stocks, bonds, etc. in accordance with the investment goals and directions of the depositor. The bank is usually given the discretion to make investments and transfer funds among investments.

Some foreign banks allow depositors to invest on margin. They can make investments by depositing only a fraction of the cost of the investment. In the United States, there are specific margin requirements for stock market purchases; currently an investor must deposit 50 percent of the amount of an investment with a broker. A foreign account which allows investments on margin may provide a way to make legal investments while not being restricted by the margin requirements in effect in the U.S.

Many banks are reluctant to announce a minimum amount which they will accept for investment management, but most do not like to accept less than $50,000 and prefer at least $100,000 in such accounts. In placing such an amount in a foreign bank, the investor should keep his or her diversification goals in mind. Most investors will not want more than 20 percent or 25 percent of their total portfolio in foreign investment instruments, so the individual would have to have a portfolio of at least $400,000 to justify placing $100,000 in a foreign bank for investment management. The individual who is willing to check with several banks, and perhaps do some negotiating, can probably find a bank which will take a smaller amount for management, but the investor should not expect to get a lot of personal attention if the account balance is only $15,000 or $25,000.

Mutual Funds

A better choice for the smaller investor is *foreign bank managed mutual funds*. Many banks in financial centers such as London, Geneva, Zurich or Hong Kong manage their own mutual funds which are available to the person with only a few thousand dollars to invest. These funds enable the smaller investor to choose a fund which has the investment objectives—income, growth, concentration on stocks of a particular country, etc.—for which the investor is looking.

Banks usually make it possible to transfer money easily from a checking account to one of the bank's mutual funds or from the fund back to the checking account. Directions for transfers can be given by wire, phone or letter. Another option is for the investor to direct the bank to move a given amount from the checking account to a mutual fund on a regular basis, perhaps so much to be invested in the mutual fund each month or each quarter. This lets the investor take advantage of the strategy of dollar averaging in purchasing the mutual fund.

Precious Metals

Most large foreign banks provide a variety of services related to investing in precious metals, particularly gold. If one wants to buy and hold gold bullion, an overseas bank will make the purchase and provide storage for it, in payment for a storage fee. The same could apply to coins. If the investor preferred to hold coins rather than bullion, a bank can arrange to make the purchases and provide storage for them.

Some banks also offer precious metals certificates. These are certificates, similar to common stock certificates, which represent a specific number of ounces (or perhaps some other unit of measurement) of the metal. The bank will sell or redeem such certificates, or if the individual chooses, he or she can appear at the bank and actually take possession of the metal.

The more aggressive investor can also trade in precious metals options or futures through overseas banks. These investment instruments, like all options and futures, involve predicting (guessing?) the price of a precious metal at some date in the future and making current purchases or sales accordingly. This is a high risk kind of investing, and it is inappropriate for all but the most experienced investors. Even then it should be undertaken only with money the investor can afford to lose.

Some investors think of owning stock in mining companies which produce and sell precious metals as a way of owning precious metals. In reality owning such shares is no different than owning shares of other companies. The price of the metals is only one, and usually not the most important, of the influences on the price of the stock. The stock price will also be affected by quality of management, profitability, price/earnings ratios and the same kinds of factors that affect the price of other stocks. Ownership of such stocks may well be appropriate, but this should be thought of as part of the general investment management services provided by a bank and not specifically as part of their services that make it possible to own precious metals.

Swiss Annuities

An attractive financial product, available primarily in Switzerland but also in some other countries. is the annuity. An investor can purchase an annuity which will be issued in the currency of the host country, Swiss francs in the case of Swiss annuities. The annuity is purchased with a single payment, $10,000 or $100,000 or whatever, at the time of purchase.

The annuity has several advantages. First, it accumulates interest on a tax-deferred basis. No taxes are due until the annuity matures and the funds are withdrawn. Funds need not be withdrawn even at maturity. They can be reinvested or they can be converted at retirement into an annuity that provides monthly payments rather than a single lump-sum payment.

Annuities are not bank accounts so they need not be reported to the Internal Revenue Service as bank accounts must. The interest earned is subject to tax but only at the time of actual withdrawal.

Because annuities are issued in the currency of the host country they are an investment in the future of that currency. An investor who believes that the Swiss franc will be stronger in the long run than the U.S. dollar can buy an annuity in hopes of profitting not only from the interest rate return but also from the gradual appreciation in the value of the franc against the dollar.

Some annuities also have an insurance feature. A portion of the return goes to buy a life insurance policy on the insured. Older investors sometimes identify a younger member of the family, perhaps a grandchild, to be insured because the insurance rates will be lower on a younger insuree.

Those interested in this investment possibility can contact the following:

Jurg M. Lattmann AG
Germanstrasse 55
Zurich
Tel: 01-363 25 10

This firm is not itself an insurance company but has information on the annuities offered by several different Swiss firms.

Financial Privacy

Ask a foreign banker what services he offers, and if he is from a country such as Switzerland, Austria or the Cayman Islands he is likely to tell you one of the most important services he offers is privacy. As noted above, this is a major motivation for many who open overseas accounts.

The laws, as well as the professional practices, of countries which take pride in their banking confidentiality guarantee the depositor a very high degree of privacy. Neither the government of that country nor of foreign nations may ordinarily gain access to information about individual bank accounts. What, you may ask, about cases such as President Marcos of the Philippines or Ollie North in the Iran-Contra affair? Didn't the Swiss government give U.S. officials access to information about those bank accounts?

To understand these cases it is necessary to understand current Swiss law. Swiss banking law provides that the government will cooperate with foreign governments in the investigation of crimes *if* the crime being investigated is a crime *in Switzerland* as well as in the other country involved. Actions such as financial fraud, trading in illegal drugs or embezzling are crimes in Switzerland so the government would cooperate with foreign officials investigating such matters.

Many investors are concerned about tax matters, and it is important to note that the nonpayment of taxes is not a crime in Switzerland. The nonpayment of taxes would be considered similar to what we in the United States would view as a civil, rather than a criminal, matter. Therefore, if that were the only issue, it is unlikely that the Swiss would cooperate with a foreign government in the investigation of it.

An additional word of caution is needed. Many foreign based banks now have branches in the United States. This gives the U.S. government considerable "leverage" over such banks. If an agency of the U.S. government wants a piece of information badly enough, it can apply great pressure to the U.S. branches of a foreign bank (through regulatory harassment, etc.) in an effort to get the home office of the bank in the foreign country to be more "cooperative" in investigating the accounts of U.S. citizens. This is not a reason to reject the idea of seeking privacy through a foreign account, but it is a threat to keep in mind. If individuals are breaking the law, it is unlikely that foreign bank secrecy will protect them in the long run. On the other hand, if a person is being sued or is in the process of getting a divorce, it is unlikely that his or her adversaries will be able to break the veil of foreign banking privacy to get information about the amount of that person's financial assets.

Service Fees

In seeking out the services of foreign banks, the potential depositor should keep in mind that these banks usually charge higher fees than will be found in U.S. banks. This is especially true of relatively smaller investors, those placing less than $100,000 in a foreign bank. The banks are also likely to pay comparatively lower interest rates on deposits which, of course, is another way of charging higher fees.

Investors should do comparative shopping if possible. Request information about charges and compare the costs of doing business at different banks. Charges should not be the only determinant in selecting a bank—the quality of services is even more important—but the level of fees at many overseas banks is sufficiently high that it should be one factor to consider in making a choice of bank.

TAX AND REPORTING IMPLICATIONS

Depositing money in a foreign account or earning income on overseas investments does not excuse an individual from tax obligations at home. A United States citizen is required to pay taxes on investment income even if those investments are overseas. Many foreign countries withhold tax on interest and dividends paid to individuals who are not residents of that country. For example, if a country had a 15 percent withholding tax, the individual expecting to receive $100 in dividends would actually receive $85.

The United States has tax agreements with most major countries to enable the U.S. resident to reclaim the dividends or interest which have been withheld by the foreign nation. In filing one's U.S. tax return, the taxes withheld abroad can be claimed as a credit against U.S. taxes.

It is important to note, however, that by claiming the tax credit on a U.S. income tax return the investor is *informing the Internal Revenue Service* of the existence of foreign bank accounts or investments. If the investor has the idea of just "forgetting" about the foreign investments in filing a tax return, he or she should keep in mind that such forgetfulness is not only illegal but it also keeps the taxpayer from reclaiming the taxes that were withheld in the foreign country. Some investors obviously consider the possible consequences and decide that such forgetfulness is worth the risk and the loss of the tax refund.

In addition to the obligation to pay taxes the U.S. investor also is required to report on certain financial transactions. One way in which the United States is one of the world's most liberal nations is in currency controls. Many governments limit the amount of money which may be brought into or (especially) out of the country. The U.S. does not impose such limits; American citizens are free to move whatever amounts of money they choose across national borders. They must, however, *report* on certain financial transactions. Whenever a U.S. citizen transfers $10,000 or more to a foreign nation, that must be reported to the U.S. Customs Office. U.S. Customs Form 4790 must be filed in such cases. If the individual is carrying the money, the form can be filed with the customs official at the border upon leaving the country. If the money is being transferred by mail or wire, the form can be mailed to the U.S. Customs Office in Washington. If smaller amounts are being moved no report is required. Note that each individual can move up to $10,000. A husband traveling abroad could take up to $10,000 without reporting it, and his wife could take up to another $10,000 also with no report required. This requirement would apply to currency, travelers' checks or other monetary instruments.

Individuals must also report the existence of foreign bank accounts. On Schedule B of the Internal Revenue Service tax forms the taxpayer is asked the following question:

> At any time during (year), did you have an interest in or a signature or other authority over a financial account in a foreign country (such as a bank account, securities account, or other financial account)?

The instructions for the tax form indicate that the question must be answered "Yes" only if the total amount in such accounts is $10,000 or more. Also, the Swiss Annuities discussed above are not bank accounts and do not have to be reported. If the answer is affirmative, then the taxpayer must also file Treasury Department Form TD F 90-22.1 which asks for more detail about the accounts.

OPENING AN ACCOUNT

The process of opening an account in an overseas bank is fairly simple. The potential account holder will want to get information about several banks in order to choose the best one for his or her needs. Actually opening the account can be done either in person or by mail.

Choosing a Bank

Choosing a bank begins with deciding which country one wants to have an account in. That will depend on many of the issues we have discussed above—business interests, investment plans, world view, etc. Later in this chapter we summarize the characteristics of several of the favorite overseas banking centers.

Having selected a country it is wise to consider several banks. The best way to choose a bank is obviously to visit the country and check out the banks personally. Ask a representative of each bank if it specializes is servicing foreign clients. Do the bank's officers and representatives speak English? Is it possible to do business by phone, wire and mail? You will want to know what services it offers to investors like you. If you are a small investor, you will want to know what the minimum deposit requirements are. If you are a larger investor, you should check on what special services are available to their larger depositors. For example, do they assign a personal account representative so that you will always deal with the same person when you contact the bank.

A potential investor will want to check on whether the bank provides the particular services that person wants. Does the bank offer precious metals trading and storage? Does it offer its own mutual funds? What are the track records of its mutual funds or individually managed accounts over the last three to five years?

It is always important to check on what fees will be charged for the services you require. As we noted, fees and charges at overseas banks tend to be higher that at domestic banks. Investors with smaller amounts of money, perhaps under $50,000, to place with the bank should be especially careful to check on this. Smaller depositors can find their funds quickly eaten up by fees if they are not careful.

Banking by Phone or Mail

Although advisable, it is not absolutely necessary to visit a foreign country in order to open an account and do business there. A person who follows world affairs carefully, for example, might decide it is important to invest in Asia for the next decade or so and want to open an account in Hong Kong to handle investment matters. If necessary a Hong Kong bank can be selected and an account opened without making a trip there.

The first step would be to get a list of several banks which do business with foreign depositors. We list banks of several nations below, and information would be available to investors at their local library. An individual could also contact the embassy or consular office of the country in which they want to have an account. Embassies are in Washington, but most major nations would have consular offices in large cities such as Chicago, San Francisco or Los Angeles.

Having compiled a list of banks, the potential investor can either write or call them for information. An overseas phone call is a bit more expensive, of course, but it has the advantage of enabling the investor to find out quickly whether the bank has representatives competent to do business in English. The questions to be asked in the letter or phone call would be the same kinds as we mentioned above for the individual making a personal visit to foreign banks.

We would add a word of caution here. If you are opening the account by phone or mail because you feel you cannot afford to visit the foreign country, that is a good sign that you probably should not try to use a foreign account in your investment activities. Overseas accounts meet many of the needs we have already discussed, but they are not for everyone. Most of this book is devoted to investment vehicles—global mutual funds, foreign companies traded on U.S. stock exchanges, etc.—which enable the average investor to develop a world view portfolio without having to use foreign banks or brokers.

NUMBERED ACCOUNTS

Numbered accounts are the stuff of which spy novels and James Bond movies are made. The common view is that a person has a bank account which is so confidential that even his bank does not know his name. All they have on file is his secret number. That is not quite the way the system works, but it that is the general idea.

Although a number of countries, including Austria and the Cayman Islands offer numbered accounts, Switzerland is the country most often associated with them. We will therefore look mainly at how the Swiss numbered account works. Even among different banks within Switzerland the procedures for opening and maintaining such an account may differ, but the principles are generally the same. The fundamental characteristic of a numbered account is not that *no one* in the bank will know the depositor's identity but rather that *only one or two senior officials* of the bank will have that information. Also, beginning in 1991 Swiss restrictions were tightened further to require that the identity of the actual owner of the account be known to the bank. Prior to that time the account could be in the name of the nominee, or representative of the real owner.

Opening an account will involve visiting the bank and meeting with a bank officer. The officer may well ask for some authentic type of identification, perhaps a passport. The officer and depositor will then agree on a number (some banks allow the use of a series of letters) to identify the account. In the future when the depositor is dealing with tellers or other lower level bank employees, only the number need be used.

The success of this system depends, of course, on the credibility of the internal operations of the bank. Most Swiss bank employees are required by bank policy to maintain the highest level of confidentiality. Even more important, however, is the fact that Swiss traditions place a very high priority on banking privacy. Even if there were no official policies, the depositor in a Swiss bank could feel confident that financial privacy would be protected simply because that is an accepted way of doing business for Swiss bankers.

As noted above, there are ways today that the U.S. government can bring pressure on foreign banks, so if an individual is using the account to hide some activity which is a crime in both the U.S. and Switzerland, it is becoming increasingly likely that the veil of confidentiality will be pierced. We doubt that many of our readers will need a foreign numbered account, but the world view investor should be aware of what they are and generally how they operate.

FAVORITE BANKING CENTERS

It is possible today to have a bank account in virtually any part of the world, including the area that we once referred to as being behind the Iron Curtain. In reality there are relatively few countries which are truly world financial centers. We will summarize the major characteristics of just a few of them. These will provide a general idea of the conditions which might be found in other nations as well. We will look at Switzerland, Austria, and England in Europe, Hong Kong and Singapore in Asia and the Cayman Islands, which are almost in our own back yard.

Switzerland

Switzerland is by far the best known of the international banking centers even though places like Tokyo, New York and London actually do more of some types of international banking. Zurich and Geneva are the major banking cities, but Lucerne, Lausanne and other Swiss cities also offer ample banking opportunities.

English is spoken by personnel in virtually all Swiss banks, and they are experienced at dealing with foreign clients. There are no exchange controls to inconvenience foreign investors. Most banks offer the full array of services—individual portfolio management, mutual funds, precious metals, checking accounts, etc. Geography is, of course, a major advantage, being located as it is in the center of Europe.

Interest bearing accounts in Swiss banks have two disadvantages of which the investor should be aware. First, because of the traditional attractiveness of Swiss banks, they do not have to offer high interest rates to get deposits. In fact, there were times in the early 1980's when they actually paid a negative interest rate, i.e. they charged a fee rather than paying interest on the accounts! Generally speaking, the stronger the currency of a country (such as the Swiss franc) the lower will be the interest rates paid by its banks, and this is certainly true in Switzerland. Therefore, you should view an interest bearing account as primarily a place to "park" your money until you decide how you want to invest it. The account itself will offer safety and privacy but little income.

Second, these accounts are subject to withholding of tax before you receive your interest payment. To recover this tax payment, you will have to apply for the tax credit when you file your U.S. income tax return for that year. As noted above, this alerts the Internal Revenue Service to the existence of the account. You will, of course, have already indicated that a foreign account exists somewhere if you have truthfully answered the question on Schedule B as to whether you have a foreign account.

If privacy is a primary motivation for opening the account, the discussion above about the increasing leverage that can be used to get information from Swiss banks should be kept in mind. This will not be a major problem for most investors, but it may be a concern to some.

Finally, it is worth noting that Switzerland is a delightful place to visit. If you want to "visit" the money in your overseas account from time to time, it would be hard to beat Switzerland as a place to do so.

The first three of the following banks are known as Switzerland's "big three" in banking. The fourth is a good smaller bank that does a lot of banking business with foreigners.

Credit Suisse
Rathausplatz
Zurich

Swiss Bank
Paradeplatz 8
Zurich

Union Bank
Bahnholstrasse 45
Zurich

Bank Leu
Bahnhofstrasse 32
Zurich

Austria

In recent years Austria has tried hard to compete with Switzerland for the accounts of non-residents. They are proud of their bank secrecy, and an Austrian banker is quick to point to the recent "cracks in the wall of secrecy" of Swiss banks. It is interesting to listen to representatives of Swiss and Austrian banks speak at financial conferences. The Austrian will compare that country's secrecy laws favorably with those of Switzerland. The Swiss will reply that concerns about Swiss secrecy are overstated and unjustified, and he will then question whether you would want to place you money in a bank in a "neutralist, socialist nation," an obvious reference to

Austria's role during the Cold War. This latter argument is probably weakened with the dramatic changes in eastern Europe.

One way the Austrians compete for funds is by paying higher interest rates. If current interest income is a major objective, that might be a reason to favor an Austrian account over a Swiss one. The banks offer a variety of services, including private numbered accounts, accounts in the domestic currency (Austrian schilling) and foreign currency accounts.

The banks do not have the experience in dealing with foreign depositors of Swiss banks (few banks do), but the larger banks in Vienna are quite sophisticated in international matters. They can offer all the services needed by the average individual investor. All of them will be able to do business in English, but you should not necessarily expect that the first person you encounter when entering, or placing a phone call to, an Austrian bank will necessarily speak English. The following are among the nation's largest banks.

Creditanstalt-Bankverein
Schottengasse 6-8
1010 Vienna

Girozentrale und Bank der Osterreichischen Sparkassen
Aktiengesellschaft
Schubertring 5
1010 Vienna

United Kingdom

London might be called the banking center of the world. There are probably more banks there than in any other city, and there are certainly more foreign banks than in any of the other major banking centers of the world. London's banks are exceptionally sound, having survived the financial crisis of the 1930's, the bombings of World War II, the energy crises of the 1970's and regular shifts of power back and forth between Conservative and Labor Governments.

Banks offer the complete range of services, with accounts being available either in the domestic currency (British pounds) or foreign currencies. Banks are allowed to offer investment services including the purchase and sale of securities and the management of portfolios. Fees and charges for bank services are generally lower than in Switzerland, but banks are similar to those in Switzerland in requiring relatively high minimum balances for investment accounts.

British law requires the withholding of taxes from dividends, but there is no similar withholding on corporate bonds or on some government bonds (known as gilts). London's banks do not have a reputation for privacy similar to that found in Switzerland or Austria, but these banks do in fact offer a high degree of financial privacy. Banks have a long tradition of providing confidentiality to clients, and there are no reporting laws requiring that accounts or currency transactions be reported to the government.

In London a "building society" is similar to a savings and loan association in the U.S. (although without the recent problems!). Investors in search of slightly higher interest payments on their money may want to consider opening an account in a building society.

Barclays Bank, Ltd.
54 Lombard Street
London EC3P 3BS

Lloyds Bank, Ltd.
71 Lombard Street
London EC2P 2BX

Midland Bank, Ltd.
27-32 Poultry
London EC2P 2BX

National Westminster Bank, Ltd.
41 Lothbury
London EC2P 2BP

Hong Kong

Hong Kong has long been the banking center of Asia, but today the dominant characteristic of Hong Kong banking is uncertainty. That is because of the impending merger with China in 1997. At that time this small area, a British colony for a century, will come under Chinese control. The treaty under which this transfer of control will occur supposedly guarantees Hong Kong a capitalistic economy for at least another 50 years. It would be an understatement, however, to say that the locals are skeptical! There is no way of knowing just what will happen when the Chinese take over.

Because of this situation, those doing business with Hong Kong banks should be cautious about making commitments that extend beyond 1997. Until then it is likely that Hong Kong will continue to be an important world financial center. The Hong Kong dollar is closely related to the U.S. dollar, so dangers of loss through currency fluctuation are minimized for U.S. investors. Hong Kong prides itself on being the epitome of free enterprise, and there are no exchange controls and few other restrictions to impede the investor.

Hong Kong banks tend to emphasize their services more than secrecy although depositors can count on a reasonably high level of confidentiality. Numbered accounts are not ordinarily used in Hong Kong. There is ordinarily no withholding of taxes on interest or dividends, although tax authorities have the power to impose a tax on extraordinarily high rates of interest payments (a power seldom used).

If Hong Kong's economic system can survive the transition of 1997, the city will probably continue to be one of the world's great financial centers. Whether that will happen remains to be seen.

The following are among the major banks available for providing services to foreign investors.

Barclays Bank International
Connaught Centre (Fifth Floor)
Hong Kong

Hong Kong Bank
1 Queen's Road Central
Hong Kong

Lloyd's Bank International
2901-4 Admiralty Centre Tower
Harcourt Road
Hong Kong

National Westminster Bank
6F St. George's Building
2 Ice House Street
Hong Kong

Singapore

Singapore has rapidly become a major financial center, and if investors and depositors flee from Hong Kong after 1997, it might well become the major financial center of Asia. There are over 100 banks on this tiny island, all competing vigorously for the business of residents and foreigners. The full range of services is available, and there are no exchange controls for non-residents.

Numbered accounts are not used in Singapore, but the country does offer a high degree of banking privacy. Singapore likes to present itself as the "Switzerland of Asia." Taxes are withheld on dividends but not on bank interest. In spite of a large majority of Chinese population in both Hong Kong and Singapore, banks in both locations commonly conduct business in English. Singapore offers a reasonable Asian alternative to Hong Kong as a banking center, and it may become even more important after 1997. Major banking centers include the following.

Hongkong and Shanghai Banking Corp.
Ocean Building
10 Colyer Quay
Singapore

Overseas Chinese Bank Corp.
OCBC Centre
Singapore

Cayman Islands

Next to Switzerland (some would say even better than Switzerland) the Cayman Islands represent the epitome of banking secrecy. This small British colony consists of three islands located about 350 miles south of Miami. Banking is to the Caymans what automobiles are to Detroit or casinos are to Las Vegas. There are over 225 banks there, representing one bank for every sixty residents!

Officials of the Cayman Islands clearly want to be seen as the world center of financial confidentiality and banking secrecy. There are no exchange controls for non-residents, and no taxes are levied or withheld on dividends or interest. The banks offer accounts in all of the world's major currencies, and the client may choose the currency in which he wants his or her account to be held.

It is obvious, on the other hand, that the Caribbean region is hardly one of the financial or industrial centers of the world. If the purpose of your account is to have it invested in stocks, bonds or mutual funds of the region where the bank is located, you probably do not want your account in the Cayman Islands. If you are looking for a place simply to keep funds in an interest bearing account while enjoying the maximum of banking secrecy, this location would be hard to beat.

The Caymans are not the only haven of banking confidentiality near the shores of the United States. U.S. residents seeking such services might also consider the Bahamas or the British Virgin Islands, which offer similar opportunities to the investor. As noted above, there are many banks in the Cayman Islands, but most do not deal directly with public investors. The following are some that do.

First Cayman Bank and Trust
West Bay Road
Grand Cayman

Bank of Nova Scotia
P. O. Box 689
Grand Cayman

Swiss Bank and Trust Co.
P. O. Box 852
Grand Cayman

AMERICAN BANKS OVERSEAS

It is quite possible to have an overseas bank account without dealing with a foreign bank. Many large U.S. banks now have offices in
London, Zurich, Paris, Hong Kong and virtually all other major financial centers. These banks offer Americans many of the advantages of overseas banking without some of the most obvious
disadvantages.

American Banking Services

The individual who has a foreign business, travels often to overseas locations or is planning to retire abroad may find that all
needed services are available through the foreign office of a domestic bank. These banks make it possible to have an account in the
foreign location where it is needed and enable the depositor to have
access to banking services "on location" in the foreign country. In
most cases the overseas offices of American banks also offer accounts in several different currencies among which the depositor
may choose.

A major advantage of U.S. banks is familiarity. Americans can
expect to find most of the standard services and procedures of U.S.
banks also in effect in their foreign branches. Transfer of funds is
facilitated since it is easy to move money from an account of a domestic bank to an account in an overseas branch of that same bank.
One can also expect to find that English will be a major, if not the
major, language in which business will be conducted in overseas
offices of U.S. banks.

Certain services may not be as available from American banks
overseas. If you are looking for expertise in investments in a partic-

ular region of the world, you may be better off to seek out a local bank. For example, if you want to invest in European stocks or a bank managed mutual fund specializing in Europe, you may prefer to select a Swiss bank in Zurich rather than the Zurich office of a U.S. bank.

The individual whose major concern is banking secrecy will not seek out an overseas office of a U.S. bank. These overseas offices will be subject to U.S. bank laws in many cases, and they will certainly be expected to respond to government requests for information, transaction reports, account reports, etc. in the same manner as the domestic branches of the bank.

Foreign Currencies in American Banks

It is now possible to speculate in foreign currencies or take advantage of high interest rates paid in selected foreign countries without having any foreign bank account at all. Some of the larger U.S. banks now offer depositors the opportunity to have accounts in several of the major world currencies. Citibank, for example, offers accounts in five currencies—Japanese yen, Canadian dollars, British pounds, Swiss francs and German marks. One advantage of the accounts is that, since they are in American banks, the accounts have the protection of the Federal Deposit Insurance Corporation.

The accounts may be used by the investor to seek out the higher interest rates available in some currencies, to conduct business in the currency or to speculate in currency fluctuations. Businesses use the accounts more often than individuals, one reason for this being that the banks often require high minimum balances. Citibank requires a minimum account balance equal to $50,000.

REFERENCES

Cooper, Marion, *The World's Top Retirement Havens* (Baltimore, MD: Agora Books, 1989).

Day, Adrian, *International Investment Opportunities* (New York, NY: William Morrow and Co., 1983).

Kinsman, Robert, *Your New Swiss Bank Book* (Homewood, IL: Dow Jones-Irwin, 1979).

Warfield, Gerald, *How to Buy Foreign Stocks and Bonds* (New York, NY: Harper & Row, 1985).

CHAPTER 4

Super Region I
North America

We assume that most of our readers are residents of North America, especially the United States, and therefore most of them will invest a major portion of their funds in North America. Peter Lynch, in his book, *One Up on Wall Street*, urges individuals to invest in that with which they are most familiar. Detroit residents should know automobile stocks; residents of Dallas should be familiar with petroleum companies. We believe the same philosophy should apply to building a global perspective into a portfolio. A resident of the United States who diversifies his or her portfolio by holding 10 percent to 30 percent overseas stocks and bonds will still be investing mainly in the United States.

A well diversified portfolio might look like that described in Table 4-1. Note that we have placed the international investments in the table in all capitalized letters to emphasize them. These are just examples of how a portfolio might be diversified, but they do illustrate how investments should become somewhat more conservative as one grows older. Note that the 30 year old has 30 percent of his or her investments in global or international mutual funds (20 percent in a stock fund and 10 percent in a bond fund), and this goes down to 20 percent by age 60.

Table 4-1 Suggested Diversification Strategies

	Age 30	Age 40	Age 50	Age 60
Growth and Income Fund	20%	25%	25%	25%
Aggressive Growth Fund	20%	15%	10%	5%
GLOBAL OR INTERNATIONAL FUND	20%	15%	15%	10%
Domestic Bond Fund	15%	20%	20%	25%
GLOBAL BOND FUND	10%	10%	10%	10%
Cash or Cash Equivalents	10%	10%	15%	20%
Real Estate and/or Precious Metals	5%	5%	5%	5%

The table also shows the importance of diversifying among several different kinds of investments—stocks, bonds, cash or cash equivalents, real estate and precious metals. A portfolio need not be invested in all of these, but it should be in several of them. It would be possible to include global investments in any of the categories. For example, in addition to the stock and bond funds in the illustration, one might invest in a world oriented money market account, a mutual fund that invests in overseas real estate or a gold fund that specializes in foreign gold mines.

The illustrations in Table 4-1 assume that you want to build your investment through the use of mutual funds. It is quite possible to use the same diversification patterns but to invest directly in individual stocks and bonds rather than using mutual funds. As you will find throughout this book, many individual stocks of foreign based companies can be purchased in the U.S., or with slightly more cost and effort, an American investor can purchase directly through overseas exchanges and brokers.

Remember too that the diversification patterns represented in Table 4-1 are not meant to be seen as the "right" figures. The best diversification strategy may be different for each individual. A risk averse investor may want to put less or perhaps nothing in an aggressive growth fund. Some individuals place great emphasis on precious metals in their investment strategies, and they would want more in that category than the 5 percent suggested in Table 4-1. Others may want nothing at all in that category.

The table is also not intended to suggest that diversification strategies should be the same at all times. If you believe interest rates are going to decline, it would make sense for you to increase your holdings in bonds. If you think the stock market faces a sharp decline, you can reduce the percentage of your portfolio devoted to stocks. The right diversification strategy for you at any given time is a matter which only you can decide.

We think it makes sense to build an investment portfolio mainly on domestic investments, so we begin our discussion of world investments with a review of U.S. markets. North American markets include those of Canada and Mexico, and we will look at those markets also. A resident of the United States will be wise to invest most of a portfolio there, not just because it is home but also because the U.S. markets remain among the largest and certainly the most diverse in the world.

UNITED STATES

Population: 251 million
Currency: U.S. Dollar

Strengths:

- still one of strongest economies in the world
- most comprehensive regulation of securities markets
- highly liquid markets
- stable, democratic government
- high living standards, high level of purchasing power

Weaknesses and Risks:

- continuing high budget deficits and national debt
- negative balance of trade
- loss of many manufacturing jobs to other nations
- diminishing role as world's financial center

The United States' economic power dominated world politics and economics in the decades after World War II. Asia (especially Japan, China, and the Philippines) and Western Europe suffered much physical destruction during the war, and the U.S. not only emerged with a strong economy, but it was strong enough to help rebuild those economies which had felt great wartime devastation. The Communist nations, led by Russia, developed centrally planned economies, but they seldom competed effectively in world markets.

Two major economic trends emerged by the end of the 1980's and early 1990's. First, it was becoming clear that the Communist economies were not working. These nations were on the verge of economic collapse, and many of them, including Russia itself, were moving rapidly toward free market economies embracing many of the characteristics of capitalism. Russia, Hungary and several other East European nations established stock and commodities markets in the early 1990's. A second important trend was the emergence of Asia and Europe as world economic powers.

Japan, Korea and Hong Kong led in the development of what became known as "the Pacific Rim." The uniting of East and West Germany into a single strong nation and economic power in 1990 was only one example of the rise of Europe as a world economic center. The creation of the European Community in 1992 will strengthen the region even more. We discuss the economies and markets of Asia and Europe in Chapters 5 and 6.

The rise of other economies means that the U.S. economy, even though it has grown in recent years, constitutes a smaller part of the total than was true in earlier years. For example, the stock markets in the U.S. today constitute a smaller portion of the capitalization of the world's stock markets than formerly, as seen in Table 4-2.

Table 4-2 World Stock Market Capitalization

	Total	U.S. Markets	Non-U.S. Markets
June 30, 1980	$2.020 Bil.	50%	50%
June 30, 1990	$9.480 Bil.	32%	68%

While United States markets constituted one-half of all value on the world's markets in 1980, they made up less than one-third of the value by 1990. This provides good reason for a U.S. investor, while investing mainly at home, to build a global strategy into a portfolio.

U.S. Market Performance

The U.S. investor has a choice of many different kinds of investments, and different ones have performed well at different times. The 1970's was a period when the investor in precious metals and real estate did well, but the stock market investor achieved very modest results. Things changed in the 1980's when the stock market moved up sharply, but investors in real estate and gold did not do as well.

The Dow Jones Industrial Average is the most well known measure of U.S. markets, although it really reflects the performance of large "blue chip" stocks rather than all stocks.

Table 4-3 U.S. Stock Market Performance
(Dow Jones Industrial Average)

Year Ending Dec. 31	Dow Closing	% Change In Decade
1959	679.36	
1969	800.36	17.81%
1979	838.74	4.80%
1989	2753.20	228.25%

These numbers show the dramatic increase in equities markets in the 1980's. The chart does not fully reflect the volatility of the markets in the 1970's, a decade clouded by the Arab oil boycott and the worldwide crisis in petroleum production. In the bear market of 1973-74, for example, the Dow fell as low as 577 after having been as high as 1031 in 1973, before the boycott.

As noted, the Dow Jones Industrial Average has tended in recent years to outperform the broader markets. Although some analysts argue that small stocks usually outperform larger ones, that has not been true recently. One likely reason for this has been the increased interest of foreign investors in the U.S. markets. It is not surprising that investors from overseas will be most familiar with our largest companies—Ford, General Motors, IBM, General Electric, etc. Because they are familiar with such stocks, foreigners are more likely to concentrate their stock purchases in those companies, thereby bidding up their prices on the stock market. There is some evidence that smaller stocks and mutual funds specializing in smaller stocks are making a comeback in the early 1990's.

At least three important events impacted on the U.S. economy during the 1980's. First, our budget deficit grew much larger. Defense expenditures went up without any concurrent decrease in expenditures or increase in taxes. Second, our trade deficit also grew very dramatically during the decade. We began to buy more from overseas than we were able to sell there. The Japanese economy surged, European economies grew much stronger, and the U.S. faced much tougher competition in the world economy.

A third event, closely related to the other two, is the general globalization of the economy. We live today in what is really a single world economy and, increasingly, a single interrelated set of stock, bond, commodity and currency markets. As noted above, the New York Stock Exchange no longer dominates world trading. Fortunately, foreign investors were willing to buy U.S. government treasury bills and bonds during the 1980's. They financed much of our national debt during the decade. As the figures show, they also discovered the American "blue chip" companies and invested in them in an aggressive manner.

This globalization had important side effects. For example, the Federal Reserve is less able to influence domestic interest rates than it once was. The Fed may lower its discount rate in hopes of bringing down interest rates generally, but if interest rates remain high in other parts of the world, interest rates may not fall. International investors will put their money where it will bring the greatest return, and they may just avoid the U.S. for a while. Should that occur, U.S. interest rates will remain high in spite of the Fed in order to attract needed capital. Globalization is also impacting on domestic anti-trust legislation. It means little to dominate the U.S. markets if companies in other countries are competing vigorously in a world market for autos, computers, banking services or whatever the product may be.

Investment Opportunities

The U.S. economy still provides plenty of opportunities for the astute world-wide investor. The U.S. investor should move on to investments in other parts of the world only after building a good foundation in a diversified sound domestic portfolio. We use the word *diversification* deliberately. Experience shows that the best approach to investing is to hold different kinds of stocks, bonds and other types of investments. As shown in Table 4-1, we consider the addition of overseas investments to be just one more kind of diversification. Geographic diversification—investments in Asia, Europe, Australia, etc.—is a further refinement of world-wide investing.

The U.S. markets offer the individual investor a greater variety of investment instruments than any other country in the world. Investment fees and commissions are usually lower in the U.S. than elsewhere. Regulation is more comprehensive and effective here. Newspapers, cable television channels and radio give the American investor more information about investments and the economy than is available in most other countries.

The are many good books on U.S. investing, and we cannot begin to cover the subject here. We offer only some general comments on how U.S. investments relate to a world-wide investing strategy. The investor should begin by being aware of how investors from other parts of the world view U.S. markets. As we pointed out, foreign investors were primarily attracted to U.S. "blue chip" stocks in the 1980's. An investor who became aware of that trend early in the decade could have profited nicely from the information.

A different trend may emerge in the 1990's. Perhaps utility stocks will be in favor, or it may be the pollution control or biotechnology stocks. As foreign investors become more sophisticated about U.S. markets, they may look beyond the larger companies and follow the example of domestic investors by seeking out smaller, lesser known companies. It is safe to say that one important ingredient of a successful investment strategy in the 1990's and beyond will be to understand how foreigners are viewing the U.S. markets and how that is likely to impact the markets.

A global economy also gives the American investor a chance to benefit from the foreign profits of domestic companies. An individual can choose to invest in U.S. companies which make a major portion of their profits from overseas sales. Pepsico, Coca Cola, Merck, Bristol Myers Squibb, Ford and General Motors are only a few of the companies which make a major portion of their profits overseas. Annual reports generally describe the amount of business a U.S. corporation has overseas, and choosing such companies gives the investor exposure to the world economy without venturing beyond the familiarity and security of domestic markets. Table 4-4 shows just a few of the companies which get most of their revenues from abroad.

Table 4-4 Selected U.S. Companies With Over 50 Percent of Revenues From Overseas

American Family Ins.	Digital Equipment	IBM
Citicorp	Dow Chemical	Mobile
Coca Cola	Exxon	Motorola
Colgate-Palmolive	Gillette	NCR
CPC International	Hewlett-Packard	Pan American

Finally, the individual investor can build a foundation of U.S. based investments by using several types of mutual funds which invest mainly in domestic U.S. stocks. Mutual funds emphasizing growth, income, aggressive growth or some combination thereof are appropriate for building a portfolio of domestic investments. The investor may want to invest in funds called balanced funds.

Balanced funds, as the name implies, provide a balanced portfolio which usually includes a major portion of common stocks but may also include preferred stocks, corporate bonds, government bonds and other investment instruments. Some balanced funds place more emphasis on income while others may lean toward growth. The exact mix of funds chosen will depend on the investor's financial goals and willingness to take risk.

Table 4-5 Selected U.S. No-load Mutual Funds

Aggressive Growth Funds
Columbia Special	(800) 547-1037
Dreyfus New Leaders	(800) 645-6561
Evergreen	(800) 235-0064
Financial Dynamics	(800) 525-8085
Founders Special	(800) 525-2440
Janus Venture	(800) 525-3713
Twentieth Century Growth	(800) 345-2021

Growth Funds
Dreyfus Growth Opportunity	(800) 645-6561
Fidelity Trend	(800) 544-8888
Financial Industrial	(800) 525-8085
Founders Growth	(800) 525-2440
T. Rowe Price Growth	(800) 638-5660
Scudder Capital Growth	(800) 225-2470
Strong Opportunity	(800) 368-3863

Balanced Funds
Fidelity Puritan	(800) 544-8888
Financial Industrial Income	(800) 525-8085
Neuberger & Berman Partners	(800) 877-9700
SteinRoe Total Return	(800) 338-2550
Strong Total Return	(800) 368-3863
Twentieth Century Balanced	(800) 345-2021
Vanguard Wellington	(800) 662-7447

Bond Funds
Axe-Houghton Income	(800) 366-0444
Benham Treasury Note Trust	(800) 321-8321
Dreyfus A Bonds Plus	(800) 645-6561
Financial Bond—Select Income	(800) 525-8085
Janus Flexible Income	(800) 525-3713
Neuberger Limited Maturity Bond	(800) 877-9700
Nicholas Income	(800) 227-5987

There are literally hundreds of mutual funds to choose from. There are actually more mutual funds available than there are stocks listed on the New York Stock Exchange. Table 4-5 lists only a few of the funds available. You will find others listed in publications like *Barrons* or *The Wall Street Journal* or in the financial sections of major metropolitan newspapers.

Each fund has its own goals and objectives, investment priorities and strategies. You should read the fund's prospectus and check its performance in independent surveys of mutual funds before investing.

Another approach to getting a balanced exposure to U.S. markets is to invest in index funds. These funds are designed to move up and down with the stock market in general, attempting neither to outperform or underperform it. They are called index funds because they will use some specific index of the market as a goal for their investment strategy. For example, the Vanguard Index Trust—500 Portfolio attempts to perform in exactly the same way as the Standard and Poor's index of 500 stocks. The Vanguard Index Trust—Extended Market Portfolio, in contrast, attempts to match the performance of the Wilshire 4500 Index. This index includes many mid-size and smaller companies which would not be found in the S&P 500 index. Rushmore also offers examples of such funds. The Rushmore Over-the-Counter Index Plus fund attempts to achieve the same results as the NASDAQ 100 index, and the Rushmore Stock Market Index Plus fund uses the S&P 100 as its target index.

CANADA

Population: 26 million
Currency: Canadian Dollar

Strengths:

- high living standards and level of education
- stable government

- generally strong commercial and industrial base
- rich supply of natural resources

Weaknesses and Risks:

- concern about foreign (mainly U.S.) dominance
  of economy
- high government debt burden
- over reliance on natural resource base in the economy
- comparatively high labor costs

Canada, our neighbor to the north, is similar to the U.S. economy in many ways and is also very much affected by what happens in our economy. Canada is a major world economy by most measures. The market capitalization of Canadian companies about equals that of nations like France and Germany. One difference (some would say a problem) is that many of the major corporations are foreign, especially U.S., owned. Ford of Canada, Shell Canada, Hughes Aircraft of Canada and Imperial Oil are all owned in large part by their U.S. parent companies.

There is genuine concern in Canada that the nation is overly influenced by "the states." Most of the population lives near the southern border where it has access to U.S. television, magazines and newspapers and is in easy driving distance of major U.S. cities. The two nations are also major trading partners, and some Canadians worry that U.S. products and brand names are too dominant in Canadian markets.

Canadian economic trends resemble those in the U.S. in several ways. Canada's economy has become primarily a service economy. Services such as finance, insurance, banking and business services now account for about 60 percent of the country's economic output. The manufacturing output is mainly construction, utilities, communications and mining. Agricultural output, as in the U.S., is declining, and logging and forestry account for less than one percent of output.

Canada also resembles our economy in the relatively greater rates of economic growth in its western provinces. Although Canada's weather would hardly qualify to be called a "sun belt," its western provinces—Alberta, Saskatchewan and British Columbia—have experienced the type of growth associated with the sun belt states in the United States. Growth has been much slower in the older more industrialized areas of central Canada in Quebec and Ontario.

Canada's economy depends heavily on natural resource industries such as mining, quarries, oil and natural gas, especially in the province of Alberta. The booming city of Calgary, Alberta, called by *Barron's* (September 3, 1990) the "Houston of Canada," exemplifies the rapidly growing economy of western Canada. With a population of only 700,000, its inventory of office space totals 31 million square feet, an amount one might expect to find in a city of two million population or more. The city benefited from the publicity of hosting the winter Olympic games in 1988, and while it has experienced the boom and bust volatility of many growing areas, the general economic trends have been positive ones. Unemployment tends to be lower than other parts of Canada, and the cost of living is considerably less than in Toronto or Montreal.

Vancouver, on the Pacific Coast, has also enjoyed rapid growth. It has experienced a somewhat controversial real estate boom as Hong Kong residents, unsure about their own future after the Chinese takeover in 1997, have rushed to buy homes and condominiums there. Local residents have become increasingly concerned that they may be priced out of their own real estate market. Like Calgary, the Vancouver region is dominated by natural resource and commodity businesses. The Vancouver Stock Exchange, discussed below, lists many of the smaller natural resource companies. The aggressive investor, willing to take some risk, may want to look to the Calgary and Vancouver areas for some of the more speculative profit opportunities in Canada.

Economic Problems

Canada will be attractive to many U.S. investors for reasons of proximity and familiarity as well as others, but the nation also faces certain problems of which the investor should be aware. As we have already indicated, the economy is heavily influenced by natural resources and commodities, and it is therefore unduly affected by world prices for such products. In recent years interest rates have been somewhat higher in Canada than in the U.S., a factor that has a generally depressing effect on the markets.

Canada shares with her southern neighbor the dubious honor of having an unusually high national debt burden. Over 35 percent of its federal revenues go to debt service, making the federal government a major competitor with the private sector for capital investment funds. Finally, observers of the Canadian economy remain uncertain about the long-run impacts of the free-trade agreement and the goods-and-services tax which went into effect in January, 1991.

Canada-United States Trade

Canada and the United States have entered into a free trade agreement aimed at removing barriers between the two nations by 1998. The Canadian business community was initially very skeptical about the pact, but it has become increasingly more optimistic as time passes.

The agreement is likely to have more effect on Canada than on the United States. Exports and imports account for about 25 percent of the Canadian economy, while comprising only about 10 percent of the U.S. economy. U.S. business interests have generally responded favorably to the idea of the agreement. Larger businesses see an opportunity to place production, distribution and retail facilities wherever they can be operated most efficiently. Smaller business, less experienced in the foreign transactions, see an opportunity to move into the global business arena in a country with familiar language, accounting practices and business operations.

Consumers in both countries, but especially in Canada, are likely to benefit. Canadian tariffs have been among the highest in the world, averaging 9 percent–10 percent. U.S. tariffs on most imported products are closer to 5 percent on average. Consumers should also benefit from increased choice and quality of products. As trade walls come down and firms are free to market their products through both countries, consumers should see greater variety in the products available to them.

One group which has not been enthusiastic about the agreement has been American agriculture, especially wheat farmers. Wheat farmers in the upper Midwest—states like Iowa, Nebraska and North and South Dakota—are concerned that their Canadian counterparts receive more government help such as research and distribution assistance. They worry that one or two years of low U.S. production would bring a flooding of Canadian wheat into the domestic markets. Whether their concerns are justified remains to be seen. Investors contemplating buying agribusiness stocks should be aware of the possible problems in this area.

Canadian Investment Opportunities

Investors can participate in Canadian investments in several ways. There are several large Canadian companies that can be purchased in the U.S., either through the direct purchase of shares or through ADR's. These would include stocks that sell on both the New York Stock Exchange and American Stock Exchange, as shown in Table 4-6. Purchase of these shares is no different than purchasing the

Table 4-6 Canadian Stocks Listed On U.S. Stock Exchanges

Alcan	aluminum
Asamera (ASE)	oil and gas
Bow Valley (ASE)	oil and gas
Canadian Pacific	transportation, resources
Cominco (ASE)	mining and smelting
Dome Mines	mining
Ford of Canada (ASE)	autos
Inco	mining
Lake Shore Mines (ASE)	gold mining
Moore Capital	business forms
Northern Telecom	communications
Nova	petrochemicals
Prairie Oil Royalties (ASE)	oil, development
Ranger Oil	petroleum
Rio Algom (ASE)	uranium, coal
Seagram	alcoholic beverages
Westcoast Transmission	natural gas

Note: ASE indicates stocks listed on American Stock Exchange. Others are listed on New York Stock Exchange.

stocks of U.S. companies through brokers based in this country. When foreign stocks are listed on U.S. exchanges, their prices are quoted in U.S. dollars.

U.S. residents can also buy stocks listed on the Canadian exchanges with relative ease. Many U.S. brokers offer stocks listed on Canadian exchanges, and the brokerage fee premium is usually less than when buying stocks on other foreign exchanges. Remember that stock listings of Canadian stock exchanges, even when they are found in U.S. newspapers, are usually listed in Canadian dollars. Among the larger companies listed on the Toronto Stock Exchange would be those shown in Table 4-7.

Table 4-7 Major Publicly Owned Canadian Companies

BP Canada	petroleum
Bell Canada	telephones, communication
Canadian Pacific Ent.	investments
Gulf Canada	oil
Northern Telecom	communications
Royal Bank of Canada	banking
Toronto-Dominion Bank	banking
Texaco Canada	oil

The Vancouver Stock Exchange is the location of many small energy and natural resource stocks. Many of them are also very speculative. *Forbes*, in a highly critical article (May 29, 1989) referred to the Vancouver exchange as the "scam capital of the world." It charged that many of the transactions there are associated with manipulation, rigged prices and money laundering. On the other hand, many investment observers see Vancouver as simply an active, dynamic market where many small, new companies get their start. Whatever conclusion you reach about the operations in Vancouver, keep in mind that all agree it is a fast moving, high risk exchange. If you have some money you want to devote to speculation with possibly high profits in a short time, Vancouver may be the place. It is not usually the place to find low risk, long-term investments.

Investors interested in keeping up on Canadian investing will find *Canadian MoneySaver* (613-352-7448) to be a helpful publication. It covers the general Canadian investment scene and is published monthly.

U.S. residents can also participate in Canadian investments by purchasing mutual funds. The following funds are available.

Fidelity Canada Fund
Fidelity Investments
82 Devonshire Street
Boston, MA 02109 (800) 544-6666

This open-end fund invests in a diversified portfolio of Canadian stocks. Its investment objective is to have at least 65 percent of its funds invested in Canada, mostly in the stocks which trade on the Toronto Stock Exchange. The minimum initial investment is $2,500, and the minimum for subsequent investments is $250. There is a 2 percent sales charge, and depending on the length of time the fund is held there may be a deferred charge at the time of sale.

Alliance Canada Fund
Alliance Capital Management
1345 Avenue of the Americas
New York, NY 10105
(800) 221-5672

This fund invests in a diversified portfolio that will profit both from long-term gains and current income. Minimum investment is $250, and subsequent investments must be at least $50. The sales charge can be as high as 5.5 percent, depending on the amount of the fund being purchased.

MEXICO

Population: 88 Million
Currency: Peso

Strengths:

- low labor rates
- oil reserves
- commitment to privatization
- close to huge U.S. and Canadian markets

Weaknesses and Risks:

- chronic poverty and unemployment
- powerful and militant labor unions
- political instability

If the Canadian markets provide familiarity for American investors, the Mexican economy and markets provide sharp contrast. Although progress has been made in recent years, the Mexican economy in many ways resembles a third world country more than it resembles the economies of its North American neighbors. The nation's population of nearly 90 million is growing more rapidly that its economy can support. Poverty, unemployment and related problems place tremendous burdens on the Mexican government

In spite of the country's problems, there are some encouraging signs. President Carlos Salinas de Gortari, elected in 1988, is committed to moving toward a market economy, controlling inflation and reducing the nation's burdensome foreign debt obligations. Major industries, such as Mexicana Airlines, have been privatized. He is currently moving to privatize the banks and to reduce regulations on the brokerage, insurance and other financial industries.

Tax and regulatory laws have also been altered to encourage more economic investment. The top marginal income tax rate has been reduced to 35 percent from 60 percent, special tax benefits for small business have been changed to enable them to merge and grow into more viable enterprises, business regulations have been streamlined and restrictions on foreign investment have been revised to make the nation more attractive to foreign capital. It is hoped that these changes will not only attract foreign capital but that they will also encourage Mexican investors who have moved perhaps as much as $80 billion to other nations to bring at least some of it home.

The President's goals will not be achieved easily. Mexico's strong and often militant labor unions are resistant to wage control measures, and they are also skeptical about the privatization movement. Some of his most serious problems are to be found within his own government and party. The PRI, Mexico's dominant party, has controlled the government for over half a century, and it is suffering with internal dissension and allegations of widespread corruption. The party has actually lost some recent state and local elections, and its ability to continue to control the national government is in question.

The economy is also heavily influenced by the role of oil in the international economy. In the 1970's and 1980's, Mexico was helped by high oil prices and hurt by low ones. The nation's state-owned oil company, PEMEX, has become a huge organization suffering from inefficiency, bureaucratic rigidity and an unnecessarily large payroll. Some have called PEMEX a large government-run welfare system. In addition, Mexico's rapidly increasing use of oil may well lead to the nation being a net importer of oil by the end of this century. Given the country's traditions and strong reliance on government, there is virtually no chance that PEMEX will be privatized.

United States—Mexican Free Trade

The commitment of the Presidents of Mexico and the United States to work toward a goal of free trade between their countries is likely to be more difficult to achieve than the similar pact between the U.S. and Canada. The economies are much more different, and Mexico has only recently moved to deal with some of its most difficult problems, as discussed above.

An important, though somewhat controversial, step toward increased trade between the countries has been the construction of the *maquiladora* plants in the cities along Mexico's northern border. These are plants built mainly by U.S. companies, but increasingly by Japanese and even some European companies as well. The companies send parts and supplies to the plants where finished products are then assembled by Mexican workers who receive very low wages by U.S. standards (high wages by Mexican standards, however). The finished product is then sent back to the U.S. or other countries for retail sale.

Tax laws of both nations encourage the arrangement. Mexico imposes no duties on the parts imported into that country for use in the *maquiladora* plants. When the finished product returns to the U.S. market, the U.S. taxes only the value added to the product in Mexico. Mexico has also eased its restrictions on foreign ownership of business to allow foreign companies to maintain 100 percent ownership of their *maquiladora* plants.

Not surprisingly, U.S. labor unions have been a major source of opposition to the plants and to the broader idea of free trade with Mexico. They see the plants as opening up a massive supply of low cost labor to compete with U.S. workers. They also complain that Mexico's plant safety and environmental control regulations are much less strict than in the U.S., thereby putting U.S. based plants at a competitive disadvantage. Not everyone in Mexico supports the plants either. Some believe it makes the economy too dependent on foreign business interests. Mexican businessmen see the *maquiladora* plants driving up wages and making it more difficult for them to compete for workers in their own country.

Whatever the concerns, the fact remains that over half a million Mexican workers are now employed in the plants, and the number is growing. Their wage structure enables them to hire the very best workers, thereby assuring high quality in their products. All three of the U.S. auto makers have plants in northern Mexico as do many clothing, computer and consumer electronics companies.

Investors should watch this trend. It is likely to expand, and U.S. manufacturing companies will either take advantage of such opportunities or compete with companies which do. Investment opportunities may also be found among foreign companies which want to reach the U.S. consumer by manufacturing their own products in northern Mexico.

The next steps to Mexican free trade will come more slowly. Skepticism remains in both countries. Both presidents are determined to achieve a free trade agreement, however, and leaders north and south of the border see economic unity as important in a competitive world where Europe and the Pacific basin are becoming stronger economic forces.

Mexican Investments

Investors should be cautious about investing in Mexico. For the immediate future such investments are likely to involve higher than average risk. As noted above, the President has taken steps to privatize airlines, insurance companies, banks and other companies. Some of these may become attractive investments, but it is too early to tell for sure.

One company which has been of interest to many U.S. investors for several years is Telefonos de Mexico, the nation's telephone utility. The company has had a generous dividend policy, and it is widely held in this country. Nevertheless, the stock trades at a very low price and qualifies to be called a high risk, high volatility stock. The company's ADR's trade over-the-counter in the U.S. Other Mexican company ADR's available include those of Cifra, a retailing firm, and Tubos de Acero de Mexico, a large steel tubing manufacturer.

The *Bolsa*, Mexico's major stock exchange, is attempting to become a major international exchange and is encouraging foreign investors to buy directly. Its total capitalization, however, is still minuscule compared with other markets (about 1 percent of the New York or Tokyo markets). Acciones y Valores (Paseo de la Reforma, Mexico City) is one of the largest and most consumer oriented of brokerage houses in Mexico. They have English speaking employees and make a priority of service to foreign clients. Table 4-8 shows some of the largest publicly traded companies in Mexico.

Americans wanting to invest in Mexico have the opportunity to purchase closed-end funds.

Mexico Fund
U.S. address:
342 Madison Avenue
Suite 909
New York, NY 10173
(212) 986-5551

Table 4-8 Major Mexican Publicly Traded Companies

Grupo Industrial Alfa	steel and petrochemicals
Fomento Economico Mexicano	food and beverages
Desc Sociedad do Fomento Industrial	chemicals
Cemex	cement
Vitro	glass products
Industrias Penoles	mining metallurgy
Grupo Industrial Bimbo	food, beverages & tobacco
Grupo Industrial Minera Mexico	mining
Kimberly Clark de Mexico	paper products
Cydsa	chemicals
Grupo Condumex	electrical
Teleindustria Ericsson	electrical

This fund has done very well in recent years, achieving double-digit percentage increases most years in the 1980's. It trades on the New York Stock Exchange. It has done a good job of reflecting the Mexican economy, which means it is volatile and carries higher than average risk. The company has paid dividends on a regular basis.

Mexico Equity and Income Fund
200 Liberty Street
New York, NY 10281
(212) 667-5000

This fund seeks to achieve both capital appreciation and current income. It attempts to have at least 50 percent of its investments in convertible debt securities, and the remainder in debt and equity investments.

NORTH AMERICAN FREE TRADE

Looking to the future, a very important issue for the North American continent is the extent to which trade agreements will make it easier for commercial transactions to occur among the three countries. As noted above, a free trade agreement is already in place between Canada and the U.S., and President Bush and President Carlos Salinas de Gortari have announced plans to establish a similar agreement between Mexico and the U.S. A highly probable next step, not too many years away, could be a three-nation agreement establishing a free trade zone throughout North America. Should that occur, it would create a free trade area of nearly 400 million people and a $6 trillion economic base at least as strong as that of the European Community.

The longer range goal will be the three-nation free trade agreement mentioned above. Investors should be alert to the fact that such dramatic change always creates economic winners and losers. Some companies will become more attractive investments. Others will falter. In the long run, free trade is helpful to the consumer, and therefore ultimately profitable to the investor. And it can be profitable to the alert investor who takes advantage of the opportunities presented by change.

REFERENCES

Barrett, Charles A., *Canada's International Trade* (Ottawa: Conference Board, 1976).

Davies, Charles, "Canada's 50 Fastest-Growing Public Companies—Growing Pains," *Canadian Business*, October, 1989, pp. 64-66.

Holstein, William J. and Borrus, Amy, "Inching Toward a North American Market," *Business Week*, June 25, 1990, pp. 40-41.

Laxer, James, *Canada's Economic Strategy* (Toronto: McClelland and Stewart, 1981).

Long, Robert E. (ed.), *Mexico*, (New York, NY: H.W. Wilson Co., 1986).

Morici, Peter (ed.), *Making Free Trade Work: The Canadian-United States Agreement* (New York, NY: Council on Foreign Relations, 1990).

Tenenbaum, Barbara, *The Politics of Penury: Debt and Taxes In Mexico* (Albuquerque, NM: University of New Mexico Press, 1986).

Wright, Harry K., *Free Enterprise in Mexico* (Chapel Hill, NC: University of North Carolina Press, 1971).

CHAPTER 5

Super Region II
The Asian Pacific Rim

The Asian Pacific Rim is no longer on the verge of becoming a major economic power—it is now. Investors who turned their back on this part of the world must now look to it for opportunities. By the end of the 1990's the Asian Pacific Rim economies will be larger than those of the European Economic Community and about the same as North America's. While in the past Japan dominated the Asian economies, this is rapidly changing. The four "little dragons" of Singapore, Hong Kong, Taiwan and South Korea, now export to the U.S. almost as much as Japan does. Moreover, the second-tier economies of Indonesia, Malaysia and Thailand offer low cost manufacturing and rapid growth as they enter the industrialized world. In the background is China, a giant with vast potential, currently held back by its oppressive political and economic systems.

There are some major trends that will affect the economics of the region for years to come. About 1.7 billion people now live in the Asian Pacific Rim, and nearly a half a billion more are expected to be added to the population within the next 20 years. Currently, about 25 percent of the population is in their 30's and 40's, the prime earning and spending years. By the year 2000 this percentage will increase to about 30 percent, providing an even larger economically productive segment of this huge and growing population.

While the aggregate population is growing, individual families are shrinking. As incomes have risen, the number of people living under one roof has fallen. More separate households are being established, as extended families no longer are forced by dire economic straits to live together. As this trend continues, and the size and age of the population grows, the number of households can be expected to rise sharply.

Also contributing to the smaller size of the Asian household is the lower birth rate. Women are staying in school longer, entering the work force in larger numbers and marrying at a later age. As their level of education has risen, the number of children born per woman has fallen. This is a trend which is expected to continue. Long treated as second class citizens, women can be expected to exert a larger role in Asian affairs as we move toward the new century.

Historically, the Asian Pacific Rim economies have been predominantly rural. This is changing rapidly as people move off the farm. For example, in 1960, 28 percent of the population of South Korea lived in cities. Currently 73 percent live in cities and by the year 2000 over 80 percent will! The trend toward urbanization is affecting all the Asian Rim countries and has both positive and negative consequences. As more people urbanize, the demand for goods and services tends to rise, increasing the structural demand in the economy, contributing to a higher growth rate. The downside is that greater urbanization means greater urban congestion. Further, much of this growth is taking place in cities without an infrastructure that can adequately handle it. Social unrest often follows such conditions.

Along with these demographic trends is the relentless effect of global information on the economics of the region. The openness and rapidity of information transfer makes consumers aware of the existence of new products and services world-wide. Traditional values and consumer wants can be expected to change as exposure to different influences increases. The implications for marketing and production are clear. A greater diversity and a faster diffusion of products within the area can be expected, with consumers demanding more options, more of everything.

There are many ways an individual investor can participate in the growth of the Asian Pacific Rim. Most global and international mutual funds have some fraction of their investments in this part of the world, so purchasing one of these funds automatically provides some investment participation. In Chapter Two a listing of these international funds is provided. The fraction of total international investments actually made in Asian Pacific Rim securities can be determined by reading the current prospectus of the fund in question.

Regional mutual funds allow you to specialize in these economies exclusively, while offering diversification among the various countries within the Pacific Rim. Funds that allow you to accomplish this end are shown in Table 5-1. These funds do not all invest in the same countries, and the mix of equity and nonequity investments differ greatly. Read the prospectus before investing.

Table 5-1 Pacific Rim Mutual Funds

Open-End No-Load
    Financial Strategic—Pacific Basin
    Nomura Pacific Basin

Open-End Load
    Fidelity Pacific Basin
    GAM Pacific Basin
    GT Global—Pacific Growth
    John Hancock World—Pacific Basin
    IDS Strategy—Pan Pacific Growth
    Merrill Lynch Pacific Fund

Closed End
    Asia Pacific Fund
    Scudder New Asia Fund

It is also possible to specialize in a specific country while diversifying within that country through the purchase of a country mutual fund. One advantage of country mutual fund investing is that the analysis of individual companies is avoided, so you can "bet on" the entire country instead of on the fortunes of one or a few companies within the country. Table 2-7 in Chapter Two provides a listing of the country funds available. Further information on these funds are given within the discussion of individual countries in this chapter.

The final level of investment is to choose an individual company and invest directly through ADR's or the purchase of an individual company's stock listed on a foreign exchange (if permitted). While the proper selection and timing of a few rapidly growing companies offers the best opportunity for quick investment gains, it is also the strategy that carries the biggest risk.

Of the Asian Pacific Rim economies, a number of them appear to offer exceptional opportunities for investment by individual investors as we head toward the 21st century. In this chapter we briefly profile the following countries: Japan, Indonesia, Malaysia, South Korea, Taiwan, Singapore and Thailand. These were selected because of their long-term investment potential along with the availability within the U.S. of one or more specialty mutual funds. These funds allow you to make a diversified investment in the selected country with only a modest commitment of money. While these countries offer a range of both opportunities and risks that will satisfy most individual investors, we encourage further research outside the countries we highlight.

Serious investors can keep up with current events in the region by reading specialty periodicals. *The Asian Wall Street Journal* and the *Nikkei Weekly* are weekly publications that provide current news stories about individual companies and countries in the region. *Asian Business* and *Asian Finance* are monthly magazines with in-depth feature articles of concern to the foreign investor. *The Far Eastern Economic Review* is yet another good source of information. Other sources applicable to this region are discussed in Chapter Two.

JAPAN

Population: 123 million
Currency: Yen

Strengths:

- highly trained and motivated workforce
- close business—government cooperation
- world leader in manufacturing automation
- high societal saving rate
- emerging domestic demand for goods and services

Weaknesses and Risks:

- labor shortage
- natural resource dependency
- unfocused international leadership
- market erosion from fierce Asian competition

The Japanese post-war economic miracle likely represents the greatest manufacturing success story that we will see in our lifetimes. From a near-zero point of industrialization in the late 1940's, the Japanese are now dominant players in the world economy. Starting with an abundance of willing workers, low cost labor, cultural uniformity, teamwork managerial styles, an absence of destructive competition, and government market protection, they were able to fashion a world leading system of production in less than fifty years.

The Japanese initially concentrated their productive efforts on mass-produced consumer durable goods that were either in the mature stage of their product life cycles or were nearing maturity. These goods included automobiles, cameras, electronics equipment and like items expected to last at least three years.

Japanese manufacturers spent large sums of money to build manufacturing systems that would allow them to compete on world markets. One key feature of their systems was the implementation of automated equipment that reflected the latest in production technology. This strategy worked perfectly for producing world-class, high volume consumer durable products which were price and quality sensitive. Furthermore, since these products already had large established markets, little money or time had to be spent on major product innovation or market development. This strategy worked remarkably well, with Japan building its capacity to the point where it now accounts for more than a tenth of the world's gross national product.

The Japanese workforce is not only industrious, but they have been willing to live Spartan lives as compared to other industrialized nations. Moreover, their savings rate is from two to three times that of the United States, helping keep interest rates low. These low rates have helped Japanese businesses modernize plant and equipment and expand operations overseas.

Compared to U.S. management, the Japanese do not reward themselves with huge salaries, pensions or golden parachutes. They also attempt to hold onto workers during economic slowdowns. This has provided them with loyalty in the workplace that has been the envy of the world.

The success of Japan has been reflected in its stock market. In the 1960's both the Dow Jones Industrial Average and the Tokyo Dow reached 1000. While the U.S. Dow is over 2000 today (it exceeded 3000 in the spring of 1991), the Tokyo Dow is now over 20,000 (it came close to 40,000 in early 1990).

This incredible rise has not taken place without controversy. There has been much said about the close cooperation between the Tokyo securities markets and government ministries. The Ministry of Finance, for example, has cozy ties to the brokerage industry, sometimes even to the point of swapping employees. Some brokerage firms have been known to sponsor stock price movements through the process of *chochin o tsukeru* or "lighting the lantern." With this approach a stock is selected that has a "story" (better earnings, a new product or a potential turnaround), then its stock is accumulated by the brokerage firm and the firm's better customers.

News stories are later leaked to the media about the stock, while at the same time brokers push the stock to customers and the brokerage firm buys more stock to aid in its price rise. After a substantial profit has been made by the brokerage house and its favored customers (who may also be members of the government), its stock holdings are quietly sold out. The public, of course, is left holding the bag. Fortunately, disclosure of such practices, along with investor caution arising from the market's retreat from overblown levels, is having a maturing effect on the Tokyo marketplace.

Investors in Japanese stocks will find it difficult to value the shares of individual companies because of lax financial disclosure rules and different ways of posting corporate earnings. Large Japanese corporations, like so many in the Pacific Rim, are conglomerates with numerous cross-holdings and wide-ranging interests. Financial accounting rules call for consolidation disclosure of only "significant" holdings. If a subsidiary has sales, profits and net assets that aggregate to less than ten percent of the group totals, its data need not be disclosed. In the U.S., complete consolidation of fully owned subsidiaries is required. What this means to the investor in Japanese equities (and most other Asian Pacific Rim companies) is that traditional investment analysis of companies based on fundamental principles is extremely difficult if not impossible to do.

As a case in point, Toyota Motor Corporation voluntarily decided to upgrade its statement of consolidation in 1989. The change from the previous year was dramatic. The number of subsidiaries covered in the consolidation rose from 13 to 26 and the Toyota Corporation's long-term debt jumped 300 percent from the previous year! Having done this, Toyota consolidation is still not complete. Over 100 more subsidiaries are still not included in the consolidated statement.

In the Japanese stock market, price to earnings ratios (P/E ratios) are typically much higher than those in the United States. While a common P/E ratio for a U.S. stock may be about 15, a Japanese stock may normally sell at a P/E ratio of 45 or higher. Two factors account for such a major disparity. First, as mentioned previously, Japanese corporate earnings are not stated to reflect full consolidation. This means that Japanese earnings are understated as compared with U.S. earnings statement. Moreover, many Japanese companies have had an earnings growth rate that have exceeded that of the United States. Investors tend to pay more for rapidly growing earnings at a given level than slower growing earnings at the same level. Finally, throughout the 1980's, interest rates in Japan were very low as compared to U.S. rates. This meant that alternative investments to stocks were much less attractive to the Japanese investor, giving a further boost to the P/E ratios of stocks. What all this means to you is that using P/E ratios to assess Japanese stock valuation is not at all easy to do. To do so is more likely to mislead than illuminate.

As we near the 21st century Japan finds itself in a new situation. Its low cost labor advantage has evaporated, and domestic markets are now opening up to world competition. Furthermore, other countries have "caught on" to the methods used by the Japanese to produce low cost, high quality products. In sum, their production advantage has narrowed as more countries are producing at world-class levels.

Along with these major changes we must add the way in which Japan interacts with the world. When Japan was an economically small country, its foreign policy was primarily a selfish one, consisting almost entirely of strategies to promote its own economic well-being. With its new status as an economic powerhouse, it is just now beginning to understand that it is expected by the world to take on international responsibilities commensurate with its economic influence.

Despite the problems Japan now faces, as it moves toward the new century new opportunities abound. With a stronger domestic market Japan will be less dependent on foreign trade than it has been in the past. Research and development efforts will keep Japan one step ahead of most of their competitors, insuring growth spurred by new technology. Continued investments throughout Asia will spread the Japanese production machine and make use of low cost labor which no longer exists in their own country. Growth in these Asian countries also offers Japan a ready and increasing market for its goods and services. As the European marketplace opens, overseas investment in this part of the world will increase, but not at the torrid pace seen elsewhere. In short, Japan will remain a financial powerhouse and the principle economic engine driving the Asian Pacific Rim. Its average growth rate should exceed that of the U.S., and the Yen, on a long term average basis, should outperform the dollar.

Investing in Japan is most easily accomplished using mutual funds. The following mutual funds are currently available.

G.T. Global, Japan Growth
G.T. Global Financial Services
50 California St., 27th Floor
San Francisco, CA 94111
(800) 824-1580

This open end mutual fund has been in existence since 1985. It invests primarily in Japanese common stocks and has an objective of capital appreciation. The fund carries a front-end load of 4.75 percent and requires an initial minimum investment of $500, with subsequent minimum investments of $100. Investors in this fund may exchange their shares with other G.T. funds through telephone instructions.

Fidelity Yen L.P.
Fidelity Investments
82 Devonshire Street
Boston, MA 02109
(800) 544-6666

This open-end fund invests in high quality Japanese denominated money market instruments and forward currency contracts matched with U.S. dollar denominated money market instruments. The value of the portfolio changes based on changes in dollar-yen relationships and interest earned by the portfolio. If the Yen strengthens against the dollar, the portfolio will appreciate. The minimum investment is $5,000 with subsequent minimum investments of $1000. You can transfer your money between the Yen currency fund and Fidelity's other two funds (Deutsche Mark and Pound Sterling) with a telephone call. Fees to buy shares depend on the purchase amount. The sales charge for less than $25,000 is

0.40%, from $25,000 to $100,000 it is 0.30 percent, and for more than $100,000 it is 0.20 percent.

Japan OTC Equity
180 Maiden Lane
New York, NY 10038
(800) 833-0018

This newly organized (1990) closed end mutual fund is traded on the New York Stock Exchange where it can be purchased through your stockbroker. It invests primarily in stocks traded on the Japanese over-the-counter market. This is the principle trading market for small capitalization emerging growth companies. While this fund offers capital appreciation opportunities, it also carries the higher risk associated with developing companies and the OTC marketplace.

INDONESIA

Population: 180 million
Currency: Rupiah

Strengths:

- natural resources (oil, gas, gold, coal, forestry, fish)
- huge workforce

Weaknesses and Risks:

- poor infrastructure
- entrenched business cronyism
- political uncertainty
- foreign investment and export dependency

Indonesia is the fifth largest country in the world with a population of 180 million. Sometimes called the "biggest unknown country in the world," it is composed of over 13,000 islands spread throughout the Pacific Ocean off South East Asia. It has a huge and inexpensive workforce that is attracting manufacturing investments from around the world.

Throughout the late 1970's and early 1980's the Indonesian economy moved forward with an annual growth rate of 7.5 percent, propelled by its large reserves of oil. In the mid-1980's the collapse of oil prices devastated the Indonesian economy. The government determined to free itself from continued dependence on oil and create a diversified and less state-oriented economy. To a great degree, they have been successful.

The government opened most industries to private ownership, liberalized its banks and let foreigners buy up to 49 percent of publicly traded companies. They also allowed foreign banks to operate and allowed them to own up to 85 percent in banking joint ventures. The Jakarta Stock Exchange, which had only 24 listed stocks now has nearly 100, with 300 more expected to be listed within a few years. These moves, coupled with the low labor rates of under $2.00 an hour, resulted in a massive inflow of investment. Japan is by far the biggest foreign investor, with Hong Kong and the U.S. being a distant second and third.

Despite their economic success, there are problems. The Indonesian infrastructure is very poor. There is a massive shortage of electricity that will put a lid on industrialization unless capacity is increased. Communication and transportation among the islands is also poor and is a stumbling block to further industrial development. Moreover, direct foreign investment must be organized through a joint venture with an Indonesian partner. Complaints have arisen concerning the cronyism that exists, with relatives of the president or other high government officials being involved in lucrative business partnership deals. If there should be a change in government, these deals could be brought under close scrutiny and the agreements possibly changed. As the current president's term ends in 1993, this could become a problem soon.

Social tensions represent another potential problem area. Indonesia is a very poor country, with the annual per capita GNP of less than $500 per year. The income gap between the business people and the impoverished millions is widening, adding to the frustration of those who eke out a living in city slums and villages. Moreover, an opening up of the economy to outside interests will surely bring with it a relaxing of internal political controls. Social instability may eventually result from such influences.

In spite of these problems, Indonesia offers the possibility of achieving rapid investment appreciation, but at levels of higher than average risk. Currently there is only one Indonesian mutual fund trading on an American exchange.

The Indonesia Fund
One Citicorp Center, 58th Floor
153 East 53rd Street
New York, NY 10022

This newly organized (1990) fund is traded on the New York Stock Exchange. The objective of this fund is capital appreciation through investments in Indonesian stocks and bonds. The small and emerging nature of the Indonesian securities market insures a high degree of volatility for this fund.

MALAYSIA

Population: 17.5 million
Currency: Ringgit

Strengths:

- low labor wage rates
- large foreign investments in manufacturing
- natural resources (logs, rubber, palm oil, cocoa, tin)
- location—easy access to the Asia-Pacific region

Weaknesses and risks:

- social and political instability
- export dependency

If social and political factors do not interfere, the Malaysian economy could be a growth machine for the 1990's. The government has rolled back the public sector through a large privatization program, has instituted stricter budgetary controls and has welcomed foreign investment through tax incentives. These moves add up to potential average real growth rates of 5 to 10 percent per year for some time to come.

Japan has been the biggest investor in Malaysia, followed by Taiwan. Japanese and Taiwanese companies have come to Malaysia primarily because of the low labor rates and land availability. Moreover, environmental concerns in their home countries have placed limits on their domestic expansion prospects. U.S. companies also have a major presence in the country, primarily through the manufacture of electronic components that are exported to the United States. The U.S. is also an important market for Malaysian raw materials, such as rubber and palm oil.

It is unfortunate that the low cost, open Malaysian economy is threatened by political and social unrest. Underlying many of Malaysia's problems is the social make-up of the country. About half of the country is composed of Malays of Islamic faith. There is some pressure by this group to require the entire country to adhere to the tenets of Islam, to create an "Islamic State." The Chinese, Indians and others of non-Moslem faith that dominate in the business community view this prospect with anxiety. Strict adherence of the entire nation to Islam would not be a benefit to encouraging foreign investment or to the growing tourist industry, let alone to the citizens of other faith that live in the country.

Over the past 20 years the government has attempted to promote a multi-racial society by involving more Malays into the modern economy. Unfortunately this has not met with the success desired. Although there are more Malays with urban professional and executive jobs than ever before, the bulk of the country's capital is owned by non-Malays. This condition, along with the religious differences between the two groups, insures a long period of strife.

The Kuala Lumpur Stock Exchange is small and the trading volume is low. Corporate disclosure is said to be at the bare legal minimum. As in so many of the world's markets, price manipulation has been suggested as occurring on this exchange. The Malaysia fund is the only closed-end mutual fund traded in the U.S. at the current time.

The Malaysia Fund
Vanguard Financial Center
P.O. Box 1102
Valley Forge, PA 19482
(800) 332-5577

The Malaysia fund invests in the equities of Malaysian Companies listed on the Kuala Lumpur Stock Exchange. The objective of the fund is long term capital appreciation. Since its initial listing on the New York Stock Exchange in 1987, the fund has been marked by large swings in price.

SOUTH KOREA

Population: 42 million
Currency: the Won

Strengths:

- hardworking, well trained workforce
- aggressive, well financed chaebols

Weaknesses and risks:

- political and social instability
- foreign trade dependency
- limited commitment to research and development
- tradition of heavy economic regulation

Historically, South Korea maintained a tradition of isolationism. After the North-South war, the country began to open its economy to the world, and has now reached the point of being the tenth-largest trading nation in the world. This rapid change of course is especially noteworthy for a country small in size and with a modest natural resource base. The dependency on trade is both the country's source of strength and weakness. International trade provides growth, yet the very same trade makes the country more dependent on the status of economic health in other parts of the world. In the 1980's Korea was blessed with three "lucky lows," the low value of the currency, low international oil prices, and low world interest rates. While these three factors helped power the Korean export boom in the past, they can no longer be counted on for future growth.

If we compare the economic structure of Korea to the other newly industrialized countries in the Pacific Rim, economic concentration stands out as the key difference. While Hong Kong, Singapore, and Taiwan have economies powered by many small and medium sized businesses, in Korea the country's "big ten" industrial conglomerate giants drive the economy. More than half of all exports come from these ten companies (called chaebols), and they yield considerable political power as well.

The success of the Korean economy is inexorably tied to the success of these companies. These concerns have a number of major strengths that contribute to their success. They possess the ability to enter new markets quickly and in a big way. The cash flow from a company's major businesses has often been used to finance the losses in a new operation for a considerable period of time before profitability develops. The Korean workforce is another advantage. Despite the television images of strikes and street demonstrations, Korean workers do work hard, are well trained and literate. Moreover, although large and bureaucratic, decisions tend to be made rapidly by strong top management. The committee decision making approach found in Japanese firms is not used in Korean firms, which speeds up the decision flow and also allows for greater risk taking.

Along with the strengths come weaknesses. The chaebols are into almost everything at the same time, thereby lacking a central focus. In some of these conglomerates we can see diverse activities such as shipbuilding, construction, electronics, and industrial equipment manufacturing which all somehow co-exist within the framework of the organization. In the past this worked well, most likely because these firms essentially produced standard models of the same goods as produced by the Japanese and the West, but at a lower price. Innovation and creativity were not an issue; low-cost high-volume production was the engine that powered them to success. As the world economy expands and global competition grows keener, it may be harder to maintain the old jack-of-all-trades strategy. A greater concentration of effort, with increased expenditures on specialized research and development, will be needed if long-term success is to continue. This will be especially evident as the Korean cost advantage continues to deteriorate owing to their rising wage rates and strong currency.

As Korea moves toward the 21st century, new markets are opening up. As Koreans share in economic success, personal domestic consumption will rise. Koreans will spend more money on cars, housing, and other goods. This will tend to lessen the economic dependence on trade with other nations. Moreover, the Korean chaebols are making a major push into Eastern Europe and Russia. Their aggressiveness and willingness to take goods out of a country in lieu of currency, will make them very formidable competitors. We would expect the average growth rate of the Korean economy to be well above that of the United States over the coming years, but below the double digit rates that were seen in the 1980s.

One major uncertainty overhanging the economy is the changing relationship between North and South Korea. It is doubtful that North Korea will rapidly throw out the communist way of life as the Eastern European nations have, and prolonged negotiations can stir social and political unrest. If an economic union of some sort develops, vast amounts of South Korean capital will be absorbed by the underdeveloped North, adversely affecting the economic growth rate in the South. Eventually, however, an economic union would result in a stronger, more dynamic and competitive Korean peninsula.

Investments in Korea are made through mutual fund purchases. The Korea fund is the only specialized closed end fund sold in the United States that invests solely in Korean investments.

The Korea Fund
345 Park Avenue
New York, NY 10154
(212) 326-6200

The objective of the fund is long-term capital gains. Since its inception in 1984 the fund has traded on the New York Stock Exchange. It typically sells at a large premium to net asset value owing to the fact that is the "only game in town" for Americans to invest in the rapidly growing Korean economy, using a U.S. based fund.

TAIWAN

Population: 20 million
Currency: New Taiwan Dollar (NT)

Strengths:

- strong individual entrepreneurial spirit
- highly trained and motivated workforce
- ties to mainland China

Weaknesses and Risks:

- natural resource dependency
- foreign trade dependency

Modern Taiwan as we know it began when Chaing Kai-shek's Nationalist troops fled mainland China to avoid the advancing communists. At that time the incomes of Chinese on Taiwan and the mainland were about the same. If we look now at the comparative wealth as measured by GNP per person, we find that in Taiwan it is about $10,000 while in communist China it is only about $350

Much of the success of Taiwan has come from their industrious small export manufacturers, aided by years of a cheap currency, cheap labor and a favorable investment climate. It built an international reputation for being an efficient and reliable producer of low and medium technology products. Unlike Korea with its few giant Chaebols, Taiwan's manufacturing base has remained fragmented across many small to mid-sized family business companies. Without the economies of scale advantage that comes from large size, Taiwan manufacturers have been unable to establish their own international marketing and distribution networks. As such, much of their exports are sold under other organization's brand names, an arrangement that offers little long-term security.

Taiwan is currently entering a transition phase. The success of the 1980's resulted in a speculative blow-off in real estate and stock prices followed by a crash. It will likely take years to return these markets back to normal volatility and price levels. Wages have risen to the point where labor intensive manufacturing must leave the island to be competitive. It has been estimated that in recent years over 300,000 manufacturing jobs have been lost because production has been moved from Taiwan to other Asian countries. Despite the loss of jobs, there are labor shortages in some sectors of the economy. The affluence of many professional people has made them choosy about where they work. This has been especially troublesome for those companies that need experienced engineers.

Adding to these problems is the poor state of the urban infrastructure. For its level of development, Taiwan has spent little to upgrade public services. In major cities traffic is perpetually clogged and the air pollution is severe. The capital city of Taipei is finally starting to build a subway which would have been inadequate ten years ago. Additionally, an explosion of violent crime and public disorder has further contributed to the lowered quality of city life.

For Taiwan to sustain its past economic success it will have to upgrade its manufacturing base. Taiwan's investment in research and development is a puny 1 percent of GNP, far below other developed countries and only half that of competitor Korea. The old strategy of building and exporting low tech products with cheap labor will no longer work. The government has tried to respond to the problem by setting up cooperative research institutes, but it is doubtful that they are capable of raising the level of R & D spending or quality of output to that found in other countries.

Despite these problems there are many bright spots. The entrepreneurial spirit of the Chinese is strong and will remain one of their most important resources. Moreover, the country is undergoing political reform which will lead to a greater relaxation of controls over economic and societal affairs.

Another positive for Taiwan's future comes from its special relationship with mainland China. As China liberalizes its economic policies, Taiwan is poised to benefit greatly from the changes. Already Taiwan companies have invested heavily in the coastal province of Fujian, and more such investments can be expected in the future. Eventually this growing Taiwan-China economic relationship could be the engine that drives Taiwan's success for years to come.

There are two closed-end mutual funds that concentrate on investments in Taiwan.

The Taiwan Fund
82 Devonshire Street
Boston, MA 02109
(800) 334-9393

This closed-end fund is traded on the New York Stock Exchange. Its primary objective is long term capital appreciation through investment in equities listed on the Taiwan Stock Exchange. Since its inception in 1986, it has sold at a premium to net asset value.

The ROC Taiwan Fund
100 East Pratt Street
Baltimore, MD 21202
(800) 225-5132

The objective of this fund is capital appreciation through investment in equity securities of the Republic of China. The fund was formed from the reorganization of the Taiwan ROC fund. There are provisions to convert the fund to open-end status in 1992 if over any 12 week period after the month of May, the fund should trade at an average discount of more than 12 percent of net asset value. To actually make the conversion, a majority of shareholders will have to approve of the change. The fund is currently traded on the New York Stock Exchange.

SINGAPORE

Population: 2.7 million
Currency: Singapore Dollar

Strengths:

- highly educated workforce
- well positioned to reap benefits from changes in South-East Asia
- excellent economic infrastructure
- location: easy access to the Asia-Pacific region

Weaknesses and risks:

- tradition of government regulation
- natural resource dependency
- shortage of domestic workers

Sometimes called the Houston of Asia, Singapore is strategically situated in the Straits of Malacca, between the Indian Ocean and the South China Sea. Among the world's 20 richest countries, Singapore has become the nerve center for Asia-Pacific's oil economy. Its deep water harbor can handle huge crude oil carriers and its refining capacity is the third largest in the world (after Houston and Rotterdam). Singapore also has the region's largest oil storage facilities and tanker repair yards. Besides the oil related facilities, Singapore has an excellent physical infrastructure. Transportation, communications, and manufacturing facilities, are superb. Moreover, Singapore's economy is well diversified with the financial and business services sectors expanding rapidly. This area of the economy, whose major players include banking, insurance and investment services, now accounts for the bulk of GNP growth. If this sector continues to expand as many expect, the city-state of Singapore may someday shed its dominant oil-based image and instead be thought of as the "Switzerland of Asia."

The government of Singapore under Prime Minister Lee Kuan Yew maintained the philosophy that government knows best. Local residents sometimes refer to Singapore as a "fine city" because of the government's approach to keeping its citizens in line. In the first six months of 1990, for example, it has been reported that 10,000 pedestrians were prosecuted for crossing streets illegally. Keeping a dog of the wrong size in an apartment, throwing a cigarette butt on the street, or failing to flush a public toilet can bring forth a government citation. Moreover, newspapers have had their circulations severely restricted for publishing information not approved of. As Singapore now moves forward toward the 21st century under new leadership, many are hoping that the role of government will be somewhat diminished.

In 1986 the Public Sector Divestment Committee was formed for the purpose of identifying companies to be privatized. Ninety-nine government-owned or linked companies were identified for full or partial privatization, and from this list 41 were eventually recommended, with a phase-in over approximately a ten year period. Sales of shares of organizations such as Singapore Airlines, DBS Bank, Telecom and Singapore Broadcasting promise to provide a number of major beneficial effects to the country. First, their sale brings money directly into government coffers, making it easier to reach annual budgeted spending targets. Secondly, by adding more issues to the stock exchange, the greater resulting capitalization adds the depth needed to attract major institutional investors. Finally, privatization allows the companies themselves to be run without the bureaucratization that accompanies government involvement. Increased efficiency and competitiveness can be expected from this fundamental change.

Currently, top civil servants receive salaries at levels equal to those in the most developed countries in the world. At the same time, the great majority of hourly workers receive pay at levels competitive with countries at a much lower state of economic development than Singapore's. The comparative advantages of the few over the many is becoming all the more apparent as this small city-state attains greater affluence. So far, the diverse ethnic groups that make up this country have managed to live together without major discord. As the government "loosens-up," there is always the danger of pent-up dissatisfaction surfacing with adverse consequences arising.

Perhaps the greatest opportunity for Singapore comes from the international collapse of communism. Its close proximity to Burma, Cambodia, Laos and Vietnam offers the potential to reap huge rewards as these countries liberalize their economic structures. Being dirt-poor, the growth potential of these countries is phenomenal, and Singapore is well postured to take full advantage of the changes. Already Singaporean companies are doing business in Burma and are forming ties in the other countries.

Closer economic cooperation with close-by Malaysia and Indonesia also offer Singapore growth opportunities. The Southern state of peninsular Malaysia (Johor) and the Raiu Islands of Indonesia have been identified, along with Singapore, as a growth triangle. This compact region provides the low cost advantage provided by the emerging countries with the sophisticated management and extensive financial resources of Singapore. It also provides a way for Singapore to manage its labor shortage problem without having to import foreign workers.

In summary, Singapore is a highly developed and wealthy nation poised to take advantage of the exceptional opportunities that are arising in its proximity. Real growth rates averaging 5 to 10 percent in the 1990's are likely. Currently, the only country fund available for investment on American exchanges is the Singapore fund.

The Singapore Fund
Daiwa Securities Trust Co.
One Evertrust Plaza
Jersey City, NJ 07302

The Singapore fund began trading on the New York Stock Exchange in mid-1990. Its objective is long term capital appreciation through investments primarily in Singapore companies. It will, however, invest up to 35 percent of funds in equities of other ASEAN Group countries (Brunei, Indonesia, Thailand, Malaysia, and the Philippines) as well as in Indochina (Laos, Cambodia and Vietnam)

THAILAND

Population: 54 million
Currency: Baht

Strengths:

- a tradition of fiscal conservatism
- low labor costs
- diversified economy

Weaknesses and Risks:

- poor infrastructure
- shortage of skilled professional personnel

After the fall of South Vietnam and Cambodia, many feared that Thailand would be the next domino in the communist plan of regional conquest. While it never happened, the period following the war was marked by uncertainty and nervousness. The private sector was confused and hesitant at making new investment commitments, and there were rumblings of discontent within elements of the military. Along with this bleak atmosphere was a weak economy severely strained by an influx of thousands of Vietnamese and Cambodian refugees. High foreign debt and balance of trade deficits added to the problems.

By the early 1980's it was apparent that Thailand had weathered tne post-Vietnam storm. The threat of a communist takeover had diminished and the economic situation had stabilized through the enforcement of a strong financial discipline. Thailand was also more self reliant in energy through the development of natural gas fields in the Gulf of Thailand.

In the mid-1980's Thailand got a boost from the escalating costs that other nations were experiencing. As labor and land prices in Japan soared, Thailand with its cheap and abundant labor looked comparatively attractive for investment purposes. Along with the Japanese, American and European companies began to invest heavily to take advantage of the favorable investment climate. Later Taiwan and Korea also recognized Thailand's advantages and moved production to this country.

Looking ahead, Thailand has the opportunity to develop a truly diversified economy. Besides the recent inflow of investment for manufacturing, Thailand has a well developed food processing industry. It is currently the world's leading exporter of canned tuna and canned pineapple. It is also increasing its exports of processed poultry and fish, and its fruit and vegetable industry is expanding its export capacity. Rice is a major crop and is a significant factor in maintaining a normally favorable trade balance. Rubber, teak and tin are also valuable commodities. Tourism is another important source of revenue with much potential for future growth. The good natured and friendly attitude of its people toward foreigners, combined with beautiful beaches and diverse historic sites make the country an attractive tourist destination.

The biggest problems facing Thailand's economic growth are the country's poor infrastructure and the shortage of skilled workers. Massive deficiencies in roads, ports, electricity generation and mass transit are placing severe limits on growth. Outside the metropolitan Bangkok area, these deficiencies are most acute. While the government is attempting to address these problems, it will take private as well as public money and many years before the deficiencies are significantly reduced. The challenge will be to find a way to deal effectively with the infrastructure without incurring a large increase in national indebtedness.

Besides the physical infrastructure problems, the shortage of skilled workers, especially at the professional level, may have a dampening influence on Thailand's economic boom. Sixty-four percent of students drop out of school between primary and secondary levels. Liberal arts degrees are preferred by college students despite the high demand for business and engineering skills. The government is responding by making plans to build five universities that will specialize in scientific subjects and is encouraging existing technical universities to expand their enrollments.

Individual investors willing to invest in the growth of Thailand can do so using closed-end mutual funds traded in the U.S. Because the Thai securities markets have substantially less volume than U.S. markets and the capitalization is concentrated in comparatively few issues, high price volatility can be expected. Information on the two closed-end funds currently traded on U.S. exchanges is given below.

The Thai Fund
Vanguard Financial Center
PO Box 1102
Valley Forge, PA 19482
(800) 332-5577

The Thai Fund is the older of the two U.S. publicly traded closed-end funds that invest in Thailand. It has been traded on the New York Stock Exchange since 1988. The objective of the fund is long term capital appreciation through investment in Thai equities.

The Thai Capital Fund
800 Scudders Mill Road
Plainsboro, NJ 08536
(609) 282-4600

The Thai Capital Fund is a newly organized (1990) closed-end fund traded on the New York Stock Exchange. Like the Thai fund, its objective is long term capital appreciation through investment in Thai equities.

REFERENCES

"Asia 2010: the Power of the People," *Far Eastern Economic Review*, May 17, 1990, pp. 27-58.

"Asia, Mega-Market of the 1990s" *Fortune Magazine Special Issue*, Volume 122, Number 8, Fall, 1990.

"Country Watch: Malaysia," *Asian Finance*, June 15, 1990, pp. 35-53.

Financial Times of London Surveys. Japan, July 9, 1990, Malaysia, August 20, 1990, South Korea, May 16, 1990, Taiwan Trade and Industry, May 17, 1990, Singapore, August 9, 1990.

Free China Review, Volume 40, Number 9, September, 1990.

"Indonesia: The Hottest Spot in Asia," *Business Week*, August 27, 1990, pp. 44-45.

"Japanese Find it Tough Abroad," *Asian Business*, October, 1988, pp. 60-68.

Koch, James V., "An Economic Profile of the Pacific Rim," *Business Horizons*, March/April, 1989, pp. 18-24.

Lam, Danny Kin-Kong, "The Neglected Market: Opportunities in Taiwan," *Canadian Business Review*, Autumn, 1989, pp. 45-48.

"Malaysia," *Business America*, February 27, 1989.

Peterson, Richard, "Scrutinizing the Inscrutable," *Investment Vision*, September-October, 1990.

"Pitching Woo at the Tourist Dollar," *Asian Business*, February, 1990, pp. 44-48.

Smyth, David, *The Worldly Wise Investor* (New York, NY: Franklin Watts, 1988).

Schwarz, Adam, "Indonesia: A Miracle Comes Home," *Far Eastern Economic Review*, April 19, 1990, pp. 40-44.

Tanzer, Andrew, "Houston of Asia," *Forbes*, May 28, 1990, pp. 124-125.

"Thailand, A Vicious Cycle," *Asian Business*, November, 1989, pp. 74-75.

Van Hien, "Special Report: Indonesia," *Asian Finance*, pp. 32-62.

CHAPTER 6

Super Region III
Greater Europe

Europe may well experience the most dynamic economic change of any region in the world in the decade of the 1990's. Certainly the economic union known as "EC 92" is matched only by the coming merger of Hong Kong and China in 1997 in terms of major structural changes which will affect economics and investment opportunities. The political and economic face of Europe today is very much the result of the three major historical events of the twentieth century, two World Wars and the Cold War. The map of Europe as we know it today had pretty much taken shape by the time peace treaties were negotiated after World War I, 1914-1918.

The financial collapse and depression of the 1930's was a worldwide phenomenon, but it was especially harsh in Europe because it was a major factor in Hitler's coming to power in Germany. Hitler's aggressive tendencies led to military attempts to extend Germany's boundaries, to overrun neighboring countries and to incredibly harsh oppression of millions of Europeans, especially those of Jewish origin. These activities also led directly to World War II.

When the U.S. entered the war in 1941, two of its three major adversaries were in Europe; Germany and Italy. Fortunately for Europe and the world, the U.S. and its allies emerged victorious, and Hitler's militarism and expansionism were defeated. After military hostilities ended in 1945, two major historic events dominated

Europe's post-war years. First, the U.S.S.R. extended its political power over eastern Europe, establishing authoritarian governments and communist economic systems in the countries of that area, effectively turning them into political satellites for the next forty years.

The second major event, a much more positive one, was the rebuilding of the nations of western Europe. Rather than demanding punishment and retribution, the U.S., through a massive economic aid program known as the Marshall Plan, helped rebuild the nations and economies of the region. The aid was available to both former allies and enemies, and it was crucial in building the firm foundation on which the strong economies of European nations are built today.

The prosperity found in western Europe today, less than half a century after the end of the war, might well be considered an economic miracle. The countries of that area are generally among the most economically advanced in the world. Their prosperity is emphasized by the sharp contrast with the nations of eastern Europe. The centrally planned economies imposed by communist leaders never worked and eventually led to total collapse in 1989. The rebuilding of these nations will be one of the major challenges of the 1990's and into the next century. It should also present investment opportunities for the alert and adventurous.

The largest and most active stock markets in the world, other than New York and Tokyo, are found in Europe. London, Frankfurt, Paris and Zurich are among the world's major financial centers. While language differences are still a significant characteristic of European nations, the English speaking investor will not find this to be a major handicap. Investors can participate in Europe in at least four ways: (1) buying stock of U.S. companies with major interests in Europe; (2) buying stock of European companies which trade in the U.S.; (3) buying mutual funds which specialize in all of Europe or in some special region of Europe; (4) buying closed-end funds which specialize in one particular country.

Table 6-1 European Mutual Funds

Open-End No-Load
Financial Strategic—European (800) 525-8085

Open-End Load
Capstone International—Europe Plus (4.75% load)
Fidelity European (2.00% load) (800) 544-6666
G.T. Global—Europe (4.75%) (800) 824-1580
Merrill Lynch Eurofund (6.50% load)
SLH Investments—European Bonds (5.00%)

Closed-End
Austria
Emerging Germany
First Iberia
France Growth
Future Germany
Germany
Growth Fund of Spain
Irish
Italy
New Germany
Portugal
Spain
Swiss Helvetia
United Kingdom

There are many U.S. companies today which receive major portions of their revenue from Europe. These would include Coca-Cola, Kellogg, General Electric and Ford. There are many others. There are also many of the largest European companies which trade on exchanges in this country. In each of the sections below we list companies of that particular country or region which can be purchased through U.S. exchanges.

For investors who want a general exposure to Europe but do not want to choose a single country, several mutual funds are available which invest in European securities. These are listed in Table 6-1. The investor who wants to invest in a single country or region of Europe but prefers not to choose specific companies may invest in the closed-end funds, also listed in Table 6-1.

In the remaining sections of this chapter we discuss the countries and regions of Europe which are likely to present the best investment opportunities over the next several years. Events are changing rapidly in Europe, especially the nations of eastern Europe, and investors should be alert to economic developments and investment opportunities which may arise after publication of this book.

GERMANY

Population: 78 million (East and West combined)
Currency: Deutsche mark

Strengths:

- highly developed industrial and resource base
- strong currency and commitment to control inflation
- well educated work force
- high levels of capital investment
- well positioned to play leading role in European Community

Weaknesses and risks:

- dependence on foreign oil
- labor shortage—need to import foreign workers
- tremendous financial needs to rebuild East Germany
- historic European fears about German dominance

Germany no longer threatens Europe with military dominance, but it clearly is a dominant economic force. Following World War II, the country rapidly rebuilt not only its cities which had been devastated by bombing but also its industrial base which had suffered the ravages of war. It regained its position as a world leader in the production of steel, chemicals, autos, ships and machinery.

As is common in Europe, the German government has played a more direct role in company management than in other parts of the world. For example, many German companies are required by law to include representatives of their unions on the board of directors, an arrangement known as *co-determination*. The government has also held direct ownership in many companies. In the early 1980's, however, Chancellor Helmut Kohl began to move the nation toward privatization by selling off the government's interest in major companies. The government has eliminated or reduced its interest in over fifty companies, including VEGA AG (chemicals), VIAG (aluminum and chemicals), Volkswagenwerk (autos), Deutschen Siedlungs und Landesrenten Bank (banking) and Deutsche Pfandbrie fanstalt (finance).

The major task facing the nation in the 1990's will be adjusting to the consolidation of East and West Germany. In 1990 the East German mark (Ostmark) was successfully eliminated and the West German currency (Deutsche mark) became the medium of exchange for the entire nation. Investors should be careful about assuming that the opening up of East Germany will present great investment opportunities very soon. It will take billions of marks to rebuild the economy of the east, and it will undoubtedly take years to accomplish.

Investment opportunities in the eastern part of the country should be viewed as distinctly long-term. In addition, money which might otherwise have been invested in the economy of the former West Germany will be needed in the east. This may even affect the U.S., as German funds that might formerly have been available for investment in the U.S. will now be needed at home.

Individual German investors have traditionally shown less interest in owning stock than has been true in many other countries. The country's strong commitment to keeping inflation low makes bonds, bank savings accounts and other fixed-income securities relatively more attractive than in countries with higher inflation rates. In addition, there has been only a limited amount of corporate stock available to the public. The German businessman has preferred to raise investment funds through bank financing or bonds rather than the issuance of stock. Many companies were developed as family-owned enterprises after World War II, and the owners have been reluctant to allow even a minority ownership share of stock to trade publicly for fear of losing control of the company.

There is some evidence that these attitudes are changing. Privatization, the nation's unification and the accompanying need for investment capital appear to have led to increasing interest in the stock market. The Frankfurt Stock Exchange is the nation's largest, although there are seven regional exchanges as well. Recent years have seen a tendency for more trading to be done in Frankfurt, with more than 70 percent of all market activity now taking place there. The number of stocks available is also increasing, but the number is still very small compared with major world markets. Less than 100 stocks trade actively on the Frankfurt market, and well over half the activity in concentrated in less than one-third of these.

Foreign investors may purchase shares listed on the Frankfurt exchange, working through their own broker, although the combined brokerage fees for doing so will be rather high. Several of the larger companies are also traded in the U.S. using ADR's.

Table 6-2 identifies major German companies which trade both in Frankfurt and the U.S.

Table 6-2 German Companies Trading in Germany and the U.S.

AEG (electrical)
BASF (chemicals)
Bayer (chemicals)
Bayerische Vereinsbank (banking)
Commerzbank (banking)
Deutsche Bank (banking)
Dresdner Bank (banking)
Hoechst (chemicals)
Siemans (telecommunications)
Strabog (construction materials)

Investors who prefer to invest through close-end mutual funds have several choices available.

Emerging Germany Fund
One Battery Place
New York, NY
(212) 363-5100

This fund invests in small and medium-size companies which expect to benefit from developments in East Germany. At least 70 percent is invested in German equities and equity-related instruments and at least 60 percent in smaller and medium-size companies.

Fidelity Deutsche Mark Performance Portfolio
82 Devonshire Street
Boston, MA 02109
(800) 544-6666

This open-end fund invests in high-quality Deutsche mark money market instruments. Its objective is to achieve stability of principal in terms of its value against other major currencies and to achieve a reasonable level of current income. Investors should be aware that currency fluctuations give investments such as this a comparatively high level of risk.

Future Germany Fund
31 W. 52nd Street
New York, NY
(800) 642-0144

This relatively new fund, created in 1990, is managed by the same firm which manages the larger, older Germany Fund (see below). This fund invests in smaller, developing companies likely to benefit from changes in East Germany and Eastern Europe.

Germany Fund
31 W. 52nd Street
New York, NY
(800) 642-0144

This fund, established in 1986, is the oldest of the German country funds. Its objective is long-term capital growth, and it invests at least 65 percent of its funds in German equity and equity-related securities, and not more than 25 percent in any one industry.

New Germany Fund
31 W. 52nd Street
New York, NY
(212) 474-7000

This fund invests in companies likely to gain from developments in East Germany and other parts of Eastern Europe. Its primary objective is long-term growth, and not more than 20 percent of its holdings will be in non-German securities.

FRANCE

Population: 56 million
Currency: Franc

Strengths:
- location at the center of western European area
- highly educated population; 99 percent literacy
- rich agricultural lands; major exporter of food
- likely leadership role in European Community
- steps taken to modernize and de-regulate financial markets

Weaknesses and risks:
- parochial and often protectionist attitudes
- possible loss of influence to Germany in European Community
- agriculture highly regulated and subsidized
- need to import oil

France has operated in recent years with a unique combination of "socialist capitalism." When a Socialist government was elected in 1981, there was an immediate negative reaction in the financial community. The nation suffered from a flight of capital, and the stock market fell sharply. Some of these fears were realized as the new government proceeded to nationalize several major industries, including most of the nation's largest banks. The government then added to the fears of the financial community by replacing the chief executives of most of the major banks with political appointees.

Overall, the worst fears about the Socialist government failed to materialize, and by the mid-1980's the economy and the stock market had recovered very nicely. The election of a conservative prime minister, Jacques Chirac, in 1986 gave business leaders more reassurance. Two important trends in the 1980's were key to strengthening the French economy. First, following the examples of the United States and England, steps were taken to de-regulate the tightly controlled stock market system and to allow more competition among brokers and financial institutions. Second, the government embarked on a program of privatizing over 80 state-owned industries.

These efforts were not without problems. The de-regulation program was marred by scandal, including one case of mismanagement of the money in the reserve fund of the Paris Bourse (stock market) itself. This fund, which existed to protect investors from fraud, suffered a loss of nearly 40 percent of its principal through illegal transactions by its manager. Also, the privatization program was, temporarily at least, almost too successful as the newly private companies competed with the government and other businesses for scarce capital. In spite of such problems, however, the French economy emerged with a much stronger position as it entered the 1990's.

In retrospect, it appears that the Socialist government actually helped the stock market in several ways. First, new tax and exchange controls made it difficult for the French to invest their funds overseas. This made more funds available for investment in the domestic economy. Also, the two favorite investments of the French—gold and real estate—became less attractive. Purchases and sales of gold were now required to be registered, thereby causing the owner of gold to lose his anonymity. The owner of real estate faced new laws which favored renters over landlords. Thus, money formerly invested in gold and real estate looked for new alternatives, and the stock market was an obvious choice.

Foreign investors, especially those in the U.S., will find that it is simpler to buy French stocks in their own country than to try to purchase directly in France. Several of the country's largest companies can be purchased in the U.S. through ADR's, as shown in Table 6-3.

Table 6-3 French Companies Available in France and the U.S.

L'Aire Liquide (chemicals)
BSN-Groupe (food, household goods)
Elf Aquitane (energy)
Groupe Bull (data processing)
LVMH (beverages and tobacco)
L'Oreal (personal care)
Peugeot Groupe SA (autos)
Rhone-Poulenc Group (chemicals)
Thomson CSF SA (aerospace and defense)
Valeo (industrial group)

Investors who prefer to invest in France through a closed-end fund can invest in the France Growth Fund.

France Growth Fund
1285 Avenue of the Americas
New York, NY 10019
(212) 713-2000

This fund invests at least 65 percent of its money in equity securities of French companies, including over-the-counter securities. Its objective is long-term growth. It may invest up to 10 percent of its funds in other non-French European securities.

UNITED KINGDOM

Population: 57 million
Currency: Pound

Strengths:

- independence and protection through geography
- highly developed financial system
- rich reserves of oil
- strong tradition of democratic government

Weaknesses and risks:

- aging industrial base
- internal political dissension, especially with Ireland
- history of labor unrest and strikes
- uncertain future role in European Community

The United Kingdom of Great Britain and Northern Ireland, as the nation is officially known, was one of the world's dominant political and economic forces literally for centuries. Since World War II the country has ceased to have a great colonial empire around the world, but it remains one of the major world economic powers. London is one of the two or three most important financial centers in the world, probably sharing that status with New York and Tokyo.

Since World War II, the Conservative Party, the party most closely associated with business, has been in power a majority of the time, but even the Labor Party, when in power, has been anti-business more in rhetoric than in fact. When the Labor Party controlled the government, it nationalized relatively few industries, although it has always been an advocate of high welfare expenditures and high taxes, which were seen by many as having a negative impact of business investment.

The economy of England (as the country is commonly known) today is heavily influenced by the strong leadership of Prime Minister Margaret Thatcher from 1979 to 1990. She was an aggressive advocate of capitalism and a strong private sector. In addition to her influence in her own nation, it is arguable that her world leadership along with that of President Reagan set the tone which made privatization a major worldwide trend in the 1980's and 1990's. She led a significant privatization effort in England, including telephones, electricity, natural gas and airlines. Her government also adopted policies encouraging government housing authorities to sell individual homes to private owners. These policies led to a higher proportion of home ownership and stock ownership by citizens than ever before in history.

The London Stock Exchange, which became known officially as the International Stock Exchange in 1987, has over 7000 stocks listed for trading, making it the largest exchange in the world in terms of number of securities traded (it trails New York and Tokyo in terms of capitalization). It is also one of the oldest exchanges in the world, having been established in 1773, 19 years earlier than the New York Stock Exchange. The exchange is international in fact as well as name, with over half the trading on a given day often being in foreign rather than domestic stocks.

Following the lead of the United States, many aspects of trading were de-regulated in order to provide for more competition among brokers and financial institutions. The exchange has also been modernized with the installation of a computerized trading system known as SEAC (Stock Exchange Automated Quotation).

Investors will find London's financial center—"The City," as it is known—to provide a positive investment environment. There are no restrictions on the flow of capital either into or out of the country, and the nation's currency is recognized around the world as a strong medium of exchange. Banks are a key player in the financial process. They can act as brokers, accept deposits from foreign residents and provide depositors the option of holding their accounts in any of several different currencies in addition to the pound. Investors have access to a wide variety of types of investments in the United Kingdom. There are many mutual funds, known as "unit trusts", available, and they offer a choice of objectives—growth, income, diversification, etc.—just as is available from funds in the U.S. Closed-end funds, called "investment trusts" in England, are also available. Many British investors place their money in "gilts," their term for government bonds. They offer the same low risk and safety associated with government bonds in the U.S. American investors wanting to invest in England can buy the United Kingdom Fund, a closed-end fund trading on the New York Stock Exchange.

The U.S. stock exchanges also give investors the choice of a large number of United Kingdom stocks which trade domestically in the form of ADR's. A partial list of these is found in Table 6-4.

Table 6-4 United Kingdom Stocks Trading in the U.S. as ADR's

B.A.T Industries (ASE)	tobacco, retailing
BET Plc	multi-industry
BTR Plc (OTC)	multi-industry
Courtlands (ASE)	textiles
Dunlop Holdings (ASE)	tires, sporting goods
Imperial Chemical (ASE)	chemicals
Imperial Group (ASE)	tobacco, foods
Plessey Co.	electronic equipment
Saatchi	services
Shell Trading and Transport	petroleum
Tricentral	oil and gas
Unilever	food, commodities

Note: ASE—American Stock Exchange; OTC—Over-the-Counter; Other stocks trade on the New York Stock Exchange.

Investors may also invest in the United Kingdom Fund or in Fidelity's currency fund.

Fidelity Sterling Performance Portfolio
82 Devonshire Street
Boston, MA 02109
(800) 544-6666

This fund invests in British pound sterling denominated money market securities. Its objective is to achieve stability in value relative to other major currencies and to achieve a reasonable level of current income. Investors should be aware that currency fluctuations can give investments such as this a comparatively high level of risk.

United Kingdom Fund
245 Park Avenue
New York, NY 10167
(800) 524-4458

This fund's investment objective is long-term capital apprecia- tion. It invests at least 65 percent of its funds in publicly traded companies of the United Kingdom and the balance in government and corporate fixed-income securities.

SWITZERLAND

Population: 6.5 million
Currency: Swiss franc

Strengths:

- Strong, well developed industrial base
- One of world's strongest banking and financial systems
- Highly educated work force
- Strong currency, highly stable prices
- Committed to strict budget and debt control

Weaknesses and risks:

- Small size
- Lack of seaport
- Uncertain future relationship with European Community
- Recent concerns about guarantee of Swiss bank secrecy

Mention international banking and finance and many people think of Switzerland. This small nation in the center of Europe has long served as one of the world's banking centers. Many of the unique services and characteristics of Swiss banks are discussed in Chapter Three. Switzerland's reputation for bank security and privacy became firmly established in the 1930's when many Europeans, especially German Jews facing Hitler's oppression, placed their savings in Swiss banks. In spite of threats and overwhelming pressure from German officials, the banks held firm and refused to compromise the privacy of their depositors.

Since World War II, Switzerland has maintained a reputation for high quality banking services as well as confidentiality for depositors and political neutrality. This tradition has served the nation well, but in recent years there has been increasing concern that bank privacy was being used to hide illegal money from the world drug trade. Switzerland has entered into treaties with many nations, including the United States, agreeing to assist in helping to apprehend drug traders and other lawbreakers. This has led some to believe that Switzerland has breached its traditional commitment to bank privacy. In fact, Swiss banks contend that they only cooperate when a lawbreaker is being sought who is accused of committing an act which would be a crime in Switzerland. For the overwhelming majority of depositors, their privacy is still fully protected by Swiss banks.

Switzerland's neutrality means it has not joined multi-country organizations to which most European countries belong; NATO for example. In the 1990's, the most significant result of this policy is that Switzerland is not a member of the European Community. It is too early to know whether this will have a significant negative impact on the country. The nation continues to have a strong highly respected currency, the Swiss franc, and a commitment to conservative economic policies, as well as a strong banking system so it is likely that Switzerland's economic position in the international community is secure.

The country's major stock exchange is in Zurich, where trading volume is often second only to London among European exchanges. The sophisticated Swiss financial system offers the investor a variety of opportunities, including stocks, bonds, mutual funds and foreign currency accounts. As explained in Chapter Three, a bank can offer all these services to clients. The mutual fund industry is highly developed. For example, there are Swiss funds which specialize in other countries. It is possible to buy a Swiss fund that invests only in Germany, Canada or even the U.S.

Table 6-5 Major Publicly Traded Swiss Stocks

Alusuisse-Lonza	non-ferrous metals
Asea Brown Boveri	electronics
CIBA-CEIGY Group	chemicals
CS Holding	banking
Nestlé	food, household goods
Roche Holding	personal care
Sandoz Group	personal care
Swiss Re Group	insurance
Swiss Bank Corp.	banking
Union Bank of Swit.	banking
Winterthur Group	insurance
Zurich Insurance	insurance

While there are many investment opportunities in Switzerland, the investor must usually deal directly with a Swiss institution to take advantage of them. Very few Swiss companies are available for purchase in the U.S. Swiss stocks also tend to have fewer shares outstanding than U.S. companies, causing the per-share price to be much higher than most American investors are used to seeing. It is not uncommon for these companies to trade at prices of several hundred or even several thousand dollars per share.

Some U.S. brokers trade the ADR's of Nestle, the chocolate and food company, and a close-end fund, the Swiss Helvatia Fund, listed on the New York Stock Exchange. Many investors will want to make their Swiss investments directly through a bank or other financial institution, and it is not difficult to do. Most have English-speaking staff and cater to foreign investors.

Investors preferring a closed-end fund may select the Swiss-Helvetia Fund.

Swiss-Helvetia Fund
521 Fifth Avenue
New York, NY 10175
(212) 867-7660

This fund, known just as the Helvetia Fund prior to 1990, seeks to achieve long-term capital growth. It invests mainly in Swiss equity and equity-related securities, and not more than 10 percent can be invested in unlisted Swiss securities.

ITALY

Population: 58 million
Currency: Lira

Strengths:

- rapid increase in industrial growth since World War II
- rapid increase in living standards since World War II
- diverse industrial base—steel, textiles, chemicals, autos, etc.

Weaknesses and risks:

- history of labor unrest
- Frequent turnover in government leadership
- continuing large budget deficits
- unstable currency

The Italian economy since World War II has been a unique combination of public and private ownership of industry. Banking, steel and oil are among the industries where there has been extensive governmental ownership. One unfortunate side-effect of the nationalized industries has been a tendency on the part of the government to use them for patronage purposes. They have been expected to provide jobs in addition to their primary objective, making it difficult for them to increase productivity and remain competitive in a world economy.

In spite of extensive nationalization, Italy also has a strong private sector, and names like Fiat, Olivetti, Zanussi and Benetton are familiar to consumers in many countries. In some cases private business has clearly benefited from governmental action. Fiat, for example, owes much of its ability to grow and develop to trade protection provided by government. Fiat also was quite satisfied to rely on a nationalized steel industry to meet its needs. Such an arrangement provided the steel industry access to capital which might not have been the case had steel companies been privately owned.

Another apparent paradox in the Italian economy has been the presence of Western Europe's most active Communist party. A number of Communists were elected to office, including the mayors of several middle-size and larger cities. Business found it possible to "co-exist" with Italian Communism because these Communists were more moderate than most, as is shown by their willingness to participate in the democratic process and run for office in free elections. The collapse of worldwide Communism in 1989 has pretty much made this a moot issue for Italian business.

Still very much an issue is the fact that Italians, both individually and in their businesses, are as determined as the French to ignore tax laws and government regulations. Tax evasion is widely believed to be a very common practice. Government regulations meant to apply to business are often honored mainly in the breach.

Like other nations, privatization has been a trend in Italy although it has been less extensive than elsewhere. Some companies, like Alfa Romeo, have been completely privatized and others have sold some stock to private owners while still remaining partly under public ownership. There are, in fact, relatively few privately traded companies in Italy compared with other European countries.

The Milan Stock Exchange is the nation's largest. It is comparatively small for a nation the size of Italy, and it has suffered from a reputation of much speculation and lack of regulation. There are actually more bonds than stocks which trade on the exchange, and a majority of those are government bonds. Most of Italy's larger cities have their own exchanges which are even smaller than Milan's. This tends to spread the low volume of trading among several locations, making it even more difficult to have a single effective market. There are virtually no foreign stocks listed on Italian exchanges because regulations make it very difficult and burdensome to accomplish a foreign listing.

Investors have relatively few options for investing in Italy. They can work through an Italian broker to buy stocks on a local exchange. Some of the larger companies available on the Milan Stock Exchange are shown in Table 6-6. They can also purchase the Italy Fund, a closed-end fund on the New York Stock Exchange. Open-end mutual funds are a relatively new investment instrument there. They were illegal in Italy prior to 1984, and funds specializing in Italian stocks were based in Luxembourg prior to that time. Since that time many domestically based funds have been established, available mainly through financial institutions such as the nation's larger banks and insurance companies.

Table 6-6   Major Stocks Listed on Milan Stock Exchange

Alitalia	(airlines)
EnimontSpA	(chemicals)
Ferruzzi Group	(multi-industry)
Fiat	(automobiles)
Generali Group	(insurance)
Olivetti Group	(data processing)
SME	(food, household goods)
STET	(telecommunications)

As noted, the Italy fund is available to closed-end fund investors.

Italy Fund
31 W. 52nd Street
New York, NY 10019
(212) 767-3034

This fund's resources must be invested at least 65 percent in a combination of Italian equity and fixed-income securities. Other funds may be invested in companies which have some operations or sales in Italy, as well as in U.S. government obligations and short-term securities.

OTHER EUROPEAN REGIONS

The nations discussed above represent the major investment markets of Europe, but there may be some other "comers!" It will take several years of the European Community to be sure just where the new investment opportunities will emerge. We will briefly suggest what some of them might be, including the Iberian Peninsula, the Benelux countries and Scandinavia.

The Iberian Peninsula

On the southwestern extremity of Europe separating the Atlantic Ocean from the Mediterranean Sea is the Iberian Peninsula where the countries of Spain and Portugal are located. These two countries, with a combined population of just over 50 million, have a reputation of being easy going, laid back countries. Democracy has come rather late to these nations, as has the modern development of their economies.

There is little heavy industry there, but what there is, is mainly in Spain, around Madrid and a few other urban areas such as Malaga. These two countries have also become favorite havens for retirees from England and northern Europe seeking a more moderate climate and favorable retirement conditions. These countries are members of the European Community (EC), a fact that offers them both opportunities and potential problems. Their low cost products now have access to a wider market, but they also face a much more competitive commercial environment. Industries are now subject to EC regulations which in many cases are more strict than the former national regulations. It is also not yet clear how effectively the industries will be in competing and whether labor productivity will measure up to the rest of the European Community.

How well Spain and Portugal do as members of the European Community is the key question in determining whether they will present investors with opportunities anytime soon. Securities trading is not highly developed, the largest exchange being the Madrid Bolsa (stock exchange). Repsol SA, a Spanish energy company, and a few of the larger banks are available in the U.S. as ADR's. The Spain Fund, Growth Fund of Spain and Portugal fund are closed-end country funds which trade on the New York Stock Ex- change. The First Iberia Fund, a similar fund trading on the American Stock Exchange, invests in both countries.

First Iberia Fund
One Seaport Plaza
New York, NY 10292
(212) 214-3334

The fund seeks long-term gains through investing in both Spain and Portugal. Usually not more than 20 percent will be invested in securities of Portugal, and not more than 15 percent will be in unlisted securities.

Growth Fund of Spain
1205 La Salle Street
Chicago, IL 60603
(800) 621-1148

This fund, established in 1990, invests at least 65 percent of its funds in equities of Spain, and the remainder is invested in fixed-income securities. Its investment objective is long-term growth.

Portugal Fund
One Citicorp Center
153 W. 53rd Street
New York, NY 10022
(212) 832-2626

This fund's investment objective is total return, to be achieved by seeking both long-term gains and current income. It is to invest no less than 75 percent of its funds in securities of Portugal, and up to 15 percent may be invested in unlisted securities.

Spain Fund
1345 Avenue of the Americas
New York, NY 10105
(212) 969-1000

This fund's objective is long-term capital appreciation. At least 65 percent of its funds are invested in equities and equity-related securities of Spain. The remainder will be in fixed-income securities, and up to 25 percent can be in unlisted Spanish securities.

The Benelux Countries

Belgium, Netherlands and Luxembourg—collectively known as the Benelux countries—stand in stark contrast to Spain and Portugal. They have highly developed industrial economies, and their financial systems are sophisticated and well able to serve foreign investors. The countries are strategically located at the center of European financial activity, between France, Germany and England. All are members of the European Community and have a high level of governmental planning and involvement in the management of the private sector. Nevertheless, all are prosperous and have a high standard of living.

The total population of the three is only about 25 million, as follows: Netherlands, 15 million; Belgium, 9 million; Luxembourg, 500,000. The nations are also small geographically. Both their industrial and financial systems are well developed. They are all centers of international commerce and depend on exports to help support their economies. In the case of Belgium, over half its total production is sold abroad.

The largest stock market in the three countries is in the Netherlands. The Amsterdam Stock Exchange claims to be the oldest stock market in the world, going back to the sixteenth century. The first company ever to trade publicly, the Dutch East India Company, was traded in Amsterdam as early as 1602. Today the Amsterdam Exchange is a modern market, listing a number of international as well as domestic companies. Over 300 U.S. companies trade in Amsterdam, making it one of the largest overseas trading locations for U.S. shares.

The Brussels Exchange is a smaller but rapidly growing market. It is highly computerized and has a reputation for operating in a highly efficient and streamlined manner. Luxembourg is quite small, but it is attempting to develop as one of Europe's banking havens, offering stability, security and confidentiality to those in need of such services. It is attempting to compete with such countries as Switzerland, Austria and Lichtenstein in the area of banking and financial services.

Banks in the Benelux countries usually offer mutual funds, as do insurance companies and privately managed finance companies. A few of the region's companies, such as KLM, Royal Dutch and Heineken, trade as ADR's in the U.S. There are no closed-end country or regional funds trading on major U.S. exchanges which invest primarily in these countries.

Scandinavia

The Scandinavian countries of Denmark, Norway and Sweden are located in the extreme north of Europe. Sweden has about 8 million population, and the other two about 4-5 million each. Denmark, which adjoins Germany, is a member of the European Community. The other two, which are separated from the main European land mass by the North and Baltic Seas, are not members.

The countries share high living standards, generally strong industrial economies and an orientation to seagoing commerce. They are often thought of as having socialist-oriented economies, with much central planning, extensive welfare systems and considerable government ownership of industry. This is especially true of Sweden, which has one of the highest tax burdens in the world. The country's tax revenues equal about 60 percent of gross national product, including state and local income taxes and a high value-added tax.

The Swedish government has been perhaps the primary example of a mixed economy, with extensive public as well as private ownership of business. In the 1970's and early 1980's there were a number of examples of the Swedish government purchasing faltering companies to keep them from going bankrupt and to save the jobs of the employees. In recent years, even Sweden has been influenced by the worldwide privatization movement, and there has been more willingness to rely on the marketplace to determine the success or failure of businesses.

Although the private sector represents a smaller part of the total economy in Sweden than in most capitalist nations, the private sector that does exist has been prosperous. The largest stock market in Scandinavia is in Stockholm, although it is small compared to other European markets. Trade barriers and investment regulations have made it difficult in the past for foreigners to invest in Sweden, but this seems to be changing.

Relatively few Scandinavian stocks trade in the U.S. Among those available as ADR's in this country are the Swedish companies, Volvo (autos), Electrolux (appliances), and LM Ericsson (electronics), and the Norwegian company, Norsk Hydro (energy). There are no U.S. based mutual funds which are oriented specifically toward Scandinavia. The former Scandinavia Fund ceased to be a closed-end fund in 1989. It became an operating company and now invests throughout Europe. It also changed its name to the Scandinavia Company. Many of the funds which concentrate on European investments include Scandinavian stocks in their portfolios.

Eastern Europe

At the end of World War II the nations of Europe were divided into two major groups, the free nations of Western Europe and the Communist nations of Eastern Europe, which were dominated by the Soviet Union. Winston Churchill described the Eastern European nations as being behind an "Iron Curtain." The split could be seen with special poignancy in Berlin, where the city itself was divided into East Berlin and West Berlin. The two parts of the city were eventually divided physically as well as politically when the Berlin Wall was constructed.

The Eastern European nations—Albania, Bulgaria, Czechoslovakia, East Germany, Hungary, Poland, Romania and Yugoslavia—varied in the extent to which they fell under Russian domination. For example, Yugoslavia's economic system never conformed precisely to orthodox Communist principles, and it also maintained a foreign policy that was to some extent independent of the Soviet Union. In Poland, the Roman Catholic Church never ceased to be a vital force in the daily lives of the people even though Communism is officially atheistic. The Church ultimately played a key role in helping bring about the downfall of Communism in Poland.

Nevertheless, all the countries established some form of Communistic economic system after World War II, and all of them developed trade policies that tied them closely to the Soviet Union. They were also joined militarily to the Soviet Union and to each other by the Warsaw Pact, and Soviet troops were stationed in most of the nations. The countries also shared the common unhappy characteristics of no free elections, no freedom of speech or press and domination by their Communist Parties, which in turn were often directed by Moscow. Communist doctrine called for their economies to be managed by extensive bureaucracies and central planning rather than by the dynamics of the free market.

Over a period of 40 years the economies of the nations stagnated, and living standards fell further and further behind those of Western Europe. In spite of widespread discontent, the people were kept in line by authoritarian means. By the late 1980's, however, a major change had occurred. The Soviet Union itself suffered unprecedented economic distress and deteriorated to even lower levels. In addition, Mikhail Gorbachev became Premier in 1985, and he took a fundamentally different position from his predecessors. He was unwilling to use his nation's declining economic and military resources to continue the domination of Eastern Europe.

Once the nations became aware of the Soviet Union's changed position it was only a matter of time until the pressures for reform and independence swept through Eastern Europe. In the summer and fall of 1989 changes occurred with incredible speed. Country after country experienced revolution and the overthrow of their Communist governments, finally culminating in the tearing down of the Berlin Wall. By the end of 1989, only tiny Albania continued to function as a strictly Communist nation, and even there changes began to be seen by 1991. The most dramatic changes were in East Germany, which merged with West Germany.

Economic change rapidly followed political change. Most of the nations announced plans to privatize industry and looked for foreign investment funds. Hungary even established the first stock exchange in Eastern Europe. Companies from around the world, but especially in Western Europe, began to explore ways to invest in the emerging free economies. West German companies as well as the nation's government assumed a special responsibility for helping their East German counterparts, a task that was simplified somewhat by the nation's unification.

What does this all mean for the investor? Are there great opportunities for profits in Eastern Europe? In the short run we recommend caution. These economies must undergo dramatic change, and they need very large infusions of new capital. They face problems of inflation, run-down plants and infrastructure and all the uncertainties of shifting to a free economy.

Only investors who can afford to invest for the long term and are willing to accept above average risk should consider investing in Eastern Europe in the next few years. For the aggressive investor who wants to commit a limited amount of funds to this area, there are likely to be a variety of new mutual funds, partnerships and other investment opportunities. They will almost certainly be advertised in the major financial publications, and you can watch for them there. As noted above in our discussion of Germany, several of the German closed-end funds identify as one of their objectives the purchase of stock in companies likely to benefit by expanding into East Germany. We still believe that "caution" should be the guiding principle for those considering investing in Eastern Europe.

The European Community

The division of Europe into eastern and western political groupings dominated the continent for over 40 years, but the creation of the European Community is likely to be the dominating issue of the years and even decades immediately ahead. The nations of Western Europe began developing a series of cooperative arrangements immediately after World War II. The North Atlantic Treaty Organization (NATO) tied them together militarily. The European Economic Community, known at the Common Market, joined their economic policies.

The policies developed through the Common Market evolved into the establishment of the European Community, known as "EC 92" because of the year of its official implementation. This agreement tied together twelve nations: Belgium, Denmark, France, West Germany (now just Germany), Greece, Ireland, Italy, Luxembourg, Netherlands, Portugal, Spain and the United Kingdom. The goals of the Community are to develop common approaches to such issues as trade, customs restrictions, travel and transportation regulations, construction regulations, etc. Within the 12 nations trade can move freely from one area to another just as is true among various states within the United States. Tourists traveling from country to country or workers wanting to move to another country in search of employment can move with equal ease.

The free movement of people, commerce and investment capital among the nations of the European Community means that common tariffs, import quotas and other restrictions apply to those nations outside the Community. The implications of this for the U.S. and other major commercial powers are obvious. The European nations present a great opportunity for markets for American products. On the other hand, it makes it more difficult to get their products through the trade barriers, and the common standards and regulations make it possible for European companies to become larger and more effective competitors.

U.S. companies have reacted by taking steps to be sure they are "inside the barriers." Large companies like the auto manufacturers have been in Europe for years. Pepsico purchased the two largest potato chip manufacturers in the United Kingdom in order to give them a presence inside the European Community. Other major non-European companies are building or buying a presence on the continent so as to be able to function inside the network of trade restrictions.

The member nations of the European Community also face a series of important policy questions. How far should the unification go? Some European leaders believe that political union should follow economic cooperation and advocate a United States of Europe. Others are skeptical about going that far. More immediately they face such questions as the possibility of creating a common currency and establishing a single European central bank to regulate financial and monetary policy. Bitter disagreement over such issues led to the resignation of British Prime Minister Margaret Thatcher in 1990.

The Community also faces the question of potential new members. East Germany, of course, became part of the organization when it merged with West Germany. Other countries of Eastern Europe and even Russia are exploring ways to get in or at least develop closer economic ties. The same is true of Norway, Sweden, Austria and even Switzerland. It is not surprising that the member nations differ among themselves as to which new nations to admit or whether to have any new members at all.

Does all this have any meaning for the investor. The answer is a resounding "Yes!" Economic trends not only in Europe but around the world will be affected by the future direction of commercial affairs on the European continent. The strengthening of the European Community as an investment "super region" will intensify efforts in competitive areas, especially North America and the Pacific Rim, to cooperate more closely and develop their own "super regions" of commercial and investment activity.

It is not possible to invest in the European Community as such. One good alternative would be to choose among the mutual funds, mentioned earlier, that specialize in investing in companies located throughout Europe. You can also select individual companies from among those identified with each country above. As time passes it will become more evident which ones are benefiting most from the new freedom of trade and commercial activity.

REFERENCES

Colchester, Nicholas, and Buchan, David, *Europower: The Essential Guide to Europe's Economic Transformation in 1992* (New York, NY: Times Books/Random House, 1990).

Hardin, David, "Funds, Investors Face Active Future in a New Europe," *Pension World*, September, 1990, pp. 14-15.

Kirkland, Richard I., Jr., "The Big Japanese Push Into Europe," *Fortune*, July 2, 1990, pp. 94-98.

Lieven, Dominic, "EC Policy Behind Socialism's Downfall, *International Management*, August, 1990, pp. 48-49.

"London's Transatlantic Jitters," *Economist*, November 19, 1988, p.87.

"Market Forces: Berlin Wall Street," *Economist*, November 18, 1989, p. 89.

Musto, Stefan A., *Europe at the Crossroads* (New York, NY: Praeger, 1985).

Starobin, Sam, "Visions of the New Europe," *New England Business*, July, 1990, pp. 18-19.

"The Strategic Implications of Europe 92," *Long Range Planning*, June, 1990, pp. 41-48.

CHAPTER 7

Dollar Averaging Strategies

Investors often make use of dollar averaging even though they may not realize they are doing so. Dollar averaging is the process of investing in a particular stock, mutual fund or other investment instrument at regular intervals. The result is that more of the investment is purchased when prices are low than when prices are high. This is illustrated in Table 7-1 for a stock market investment.

Table 7-1 Dollar Averaging Purchases of ABC Company Stock

$20 Monthly Investments

Month	Price of ABC Stock	Monthly Investment	Shares Purchased
January	$5	$20	4
February	4	20	5
March	2	20	10
April	4	20	5
May	5	20	4
June	8	20	2.5
Totals		$120	30.5

Average share price over six months - $4.67
Average cost of shares purchased - $3.93

The investor here is investing $20 every month in the stock of ABC Company. We are assuming for purposes of the example that one may buy fractional shares, which in fact is the case with mutual funds. It is obvious that $20 purchases more shares when the price is low than when it is high. The investor's $20 bought 10 shares in March, when the price was $2 per share, but only 2.5 shares in June, when the price had risen to $8 a share.

We can see from the example that the average price of a share of stock over the six month period was $4.67. However, the process of dollar averaging, i.e., buying more shares when the price is low, enabled the investor to buy his 30.5 shares at an average cost of only $3.93 per share.

DOLLAR AVERAGING PHILOSOPHY

Dollar averaging allows you to make investments throughout your earnings years without having to consider the current state of the economy of a country or its marketplace. It can be used on any investment vehicle, including stocks, bonds, precious metals and even real estate. The only restriction is that the size of your periodic investment is large enough to make a purchase.

The principle of dollar averaging is based on two fundamental assumptions. The first is that the long term trend of the investment is up. This has certainly been true for stocks and bonds in the U.S. Throughout the 20th century, when we have had rather accurate measures of U.S. stock market movement, the average annual rise in the market has been between nine and ten percent. During the same period U.S. bonds have also appreciated, although at about half the rate as stocks. Of course, other countries have had different rates of growth. It is not unreasonable to assume that in many parts of the world, positive future growth rates will be seen in securities markets, as well as other markets where investments can be made.

A long-term increase in the value of an investment is very important to the concept of dollar averaging. One would obviously not want to invest month after month, year after year, in any investment instrument whose long term price trend is down. While the fact that markets have gone up in the past does not guarantee they will do so in the future, it is still a reasonable assumption on which to build an investment strategy. It is also an assumption that will likely hold for any capitalist country undergoing long-term growth.

The second assumption is that the price of any specific investment instrument will fluctuate. While the long-term price trend may be up, the price will not move in a straight-line upwardly direction. There will be quite significant short term ups and downs in the price. One can expect that certain investments, such as international equities, will be more volatile than many other investments. It is this price fluctuation what allows dollar averaging to work. The price needs to go down sometimes as well as up so that more shares can be purchased at the lower prices.

If these two assumptions, that there will be short term price fluctuations but the long term price trend will rise, are correct, the investor can profit by using a strategy based on dollar averaging.

USING DOLLAR AVERAGING

The most straightforward approach to using dollar averaging is to make equal investments on a periodic basis (for example, monthly) into your chosen financial instruments. This approach will insure, if the stated assumptions hold in the future, that benefits from the approach will accrue. The active investor can, however, use a more sophisticated strategy that will make dollar averaging an even more powerful investment tool. Such a plan is described below.

While the plan may seem complicated at first, it really is not. The approach is based on the simple principle of increasing the percentage of the periodic contribution that goes into an investment as the price of that investment falls. Conversely, as the price rises, the percentage of monthly contribution going into the investment is reduced. The plan is implemented as follows:

Step 1: Begin by selecting an investment. If you wish to use more than one investment or investment type, apply the dollar averaging system to each one separately. Establish your periodic investments (we'll assume monthly into an equity investment) at 50 percent in the equity investment and 50 percent in a money market fund. At the end of the first month, note the closing price of the equity investment. That becomes your first *base price*. The base price is used for one purpose—when the price of the equity investment falls at least 10 percent from the base price, you change your monthly allocations so that more of your money is going to buy the equity investment.

Step 2: Once each month, record the latest closing price of the equity investment. Keep a permanent record of these monthly closing prices. Then do one of four things:

(a) If the closing price is above the current base price, set the new closing price as your new base price.

   Example: Last month the investment closed at $20.00. This month it closes at $20.50. $20.50 becomes your new base price.

(b) If the closing price has fallen to a level at least 10 percent below your base price, call and adjust your monthly allocations. Shift from the 50/50 allocation so that 60 percent now goes into the equity investment and 40 percent into the money market fund. Make NO adjustment in the investment accumulations in your account; only in the monthly allocations of new investment money.

   Example: Your base price, which may have been set one month ago or many months ago, is $20.50. This month your fund falls to $18.30. Since any price below $18.45 (20.50 minus 2.05) represents a decline of more than 10 percent from the base price, adjust your monthly allocations to 60 percent for the equity investment and 40 percent for the money market fund.

   Note: In succeeding months, the fund price may decline even more or it may go back up slightly. Remember that you just leave the allocations at 60/40. You do not change the 60/40 allocations until the price returns to at least the base price, as explained in (c).

(c) If you have been allocating your money on a 60/40 basis, and the price of the equity fund rises to at least the base price, return your allocation figures to 50/50. At this point you will also have a new base price to record.

Example: For several months you have been allocating your money on a 60/40 basis. Your base price through these months has been $20.50. Now your fund has moved up in price and closes this month at $21.25. Adjust your monthly allocation percentages back to 50/50. Then record $21.25 as your new base price.

(d) If your investment stays the same or declines in price but does not reach a figure at least 10 percent below the current base price, do nothing. Also, if you have already adjusted the allocations to 60/40, and the price does not rise at least to the base price, do nothing.

Example: Your current base price is $20.50. The closing price of the investment for the current month is $19.10. This is above the figure of $18.45, which would represent a decline of 10 percent from the base price, so just do nothing.

Table 7-2 shows one year of activities using this plan. The right-hand column shows which of the steps outlined above are illustrated by that month's action. Most funds would not be this volatile, but we have exaggerated the price movements to illustrate the various steps taken in implementing the strategy.

You may want to keep a chart of this type for your own use. It is a good way to keep a record of the current month's closing price, the base price and the actions taken in regard to the monthly allocations. As you keep the record month-by-month, you will become familiar with the system and it will not seem complicated at all.

DOLLAR AVERAGING ALTERNATIVES

This plan can be modified in various ways. An investor with higher risk tolerance might set the original monthly allocations at 60 percent to an equity investment and 40 percent to the money market fund. Then when the price declines more than 10 percent below the base price, the allocations would be adjusted to 70 percent for the equity fund and 30 percent for the money market fund. The 60/40 allocations, rather than 50/50, become the figures to which the plan reverts when the closing price rises back to the level of the base price.

Table 7-2 Implementing the Dollar Averaging Strategy

Month	Closing Price	Base Price	Base Price Less 10%	Monthly Allocations Equity/ Money Mkt	Action Taken	Example of Plan Step *
Jan.	$20.00	$20.00	$18.00	50/50	Allocations set	
Feb.	20.50	20.50	18.45	50/50	Base price adjusted	a)
Mar.	19.10	20.50	18.45	50/50	No action taken	d)
Apr.	18.30	20.50	18.45	60/40	Allocations adjusted	b)
May	17.90	20.50	18.45	60/40	No action	d)
Jun.	16.40	20.50	18.45	60/40	No action	d)
Jul.	18.50	20.50	18.45	60/40	No action	d)
Aug.	19.75	20.50	18.45	60/40	No action	d)
Sep.	21.25	21.25	19.12	50/50	Alloc. & base adjusted	c)
Oct.	22.00	22.00	19.80	50/50	Base price adjusted	a)
Nov.	20.25	22.00	19.80	50/50	No action	d)
Dec.	19.40	22.00	19.80	60/40	Allocation adjusted	b)

*Letters in right-hand column indicate which of the steps (a through d) described above are illustrated by that month's action.

A more risk averse investor can begin with allocations of 40 percent for the equity fund and 60 percent for the money market fund, and then adjust to 50/50 when the price declines. With this approach, the low risk investor will never have more than 50 percent of the monthly contributions going into equity funds.

COMBINING STRATEGIES

Dollar averaging strategies work through changes in the monthly allocations. They do not make changes in the investment accumulations. An investor might want to combine dollar averaging with one of the asset allocation strategies discussed in the next chapter. For example, one could use a permanent asset allocation strategy as the primary investment management approach. The dollar averaging strategy would be used throughout the year, "within" the asset allocation approach.

REVERSE DOLLAR AVERAGING

So far our discussion has focused on putting money into an investment vehicle using the dollar averaging strategy. Now we will discuss the reverse task, getting your money out. Again, the dollar averaging approach represents a viable alternative for successfully completing this task. The advantage of dollar averaging out of an investment is that the current status of the marketplace will have a diminished effect on the results of the withdrawal.

As long as you do not need all of your money out of an investment suddenly, you can make plans to withdraw it in a gradual manner. Such a gradual withdrawal, when done on a periodic basis, represents the opposite of dollar cost averaging into the investment. By easing your money out of the market you reduce the risk of selling out at an inopportune time. Moreover, by planning to phase out of your investment, you avoid the problem of being "panicked out" at the very bottom of a price drop. Figure 7-1 shows the overall dollar averaging-in and dollar averaging-out process.

Just as there are many ways to dollar average into an investment, there are also many ways that you can dollar average out of an investment. The following discussion provides details for the major approaches which you can take.

The simplest way to dollar average out of an investment is to remove the same amount of money each period until the investment is exhausted. If the investment is to be liquidated within a relatively short period of time, for example, three months, then an approximately equal amount could be sold each month until all the money has been removed. One way to do this would be to divide the total amount by four to arrive at a withdrawal amount. This amount would be sold now, again in one month, again in two months, then again at the end of the third month. This would provide for exactly equal payments from the investment, but only if the investment did not change during the time of the withdrawal. If

Figure 7-1   Total Dollar Averaging

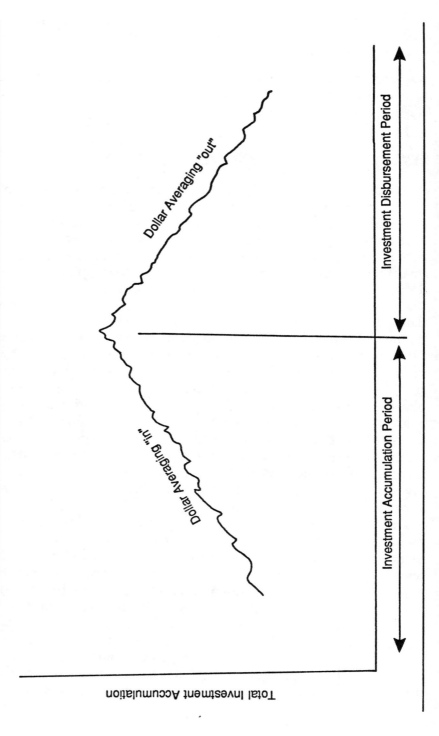

it did, then the final withdrawal will be greater (or less as the case may be) than the other payments, possibly substantially so. To counter this possibility a percentage withdrawal approach is typically taken. One-fourth could be sold immediately, one-third of what is left could be sold at the end of one month, half of what is then left at the end of two months, and all the rest at the end of the last month. This would provide an approximately equal "bite" for each of the withdrawals, with less of a chance of a surprise when the last sale is made.

If the withdrawals are to be made over a long period of time, to provide an income in retirement, for example, then a different strategy is necessary. If you know for how long you wish to make withdrawals, a compound interest rate table can be of great use. Table 7-3 shows a 20 year depletion range for monthly withdrawals at investment interest rates ranging from 4 percent to 18 percent.

Assume that you have $187,000 in an international bond fund that you believe can average about an eight percent annual appreciation in the foreseeable future. How much can you withdraw each month if you wish to have an income from this source for 20 years? Using Table 7-3, you go down the 8 percent column until it intersects with the 20 year row. You will find at the intersection the figure $8.19. This means that every $1,000 will provide a monthly income of $8.19. Since you have $187,000, multiply the $8.19 times 187, and you will find that you can withdraw $1531.53 each month for the 20 years. Of course this figure assumes an exact interest rate of eight percent, with monthly compounding. While it is naive to believe that anyone can accurately predict an interest rate 20 years into the future, this table can still be used to provide "ballpark" numbers. Every few years you can readjust the monthly amount to withdraw based on interest rate expectations current at that time.

Another way to determine amounts to withdraw is shown in Table 7-4. In this table, annual rates of withdrawal and annual rates of return can be tested to see how long the investment principle will last.

Table 7-3 Monthly Withdrawals to Deplete a $1,000 Fund

Years to Depletion	Annual Interest rate, monthly compounding				
	6%	8%	10%	12%	14%
1	$85.99	$86.66	$87.72	$88.56	$89.40
2	44.25	45.10	45.95	46.79	47.62
3	30.35	31.21	32.07	32.92	33.78
4	23.41	24.28	25.16	26.03	26.91
5	19.26	20.14	21.04	21.94	22.84
6	16.50	17.40	18.31	19.22	20.17
7	14.53	15.45	16.38	17.33	18.29
8	13.06	14.00	14.95	15.92	16.91
9	11.93	12.87	13.85	14.84	15.85
10	11.02	11.99	12.98	13.99	15.03
11	10.29	11.27	12.28	13.32	14.38
12	9.68	10.67	11.70	12.77	13.85
13	9.16	10.18	11.23	12.31	13.42
14	8.73	9.76	10.82	11.93	13.07
15	8.35	9.40	10.48	11.61	12.77
16	8.03	9.09	10.19	11.33	12.52
17	7.74	8.82	9.94	11.11	12.31
18	7.49	8.58	9.72	10.91	12.13
19	7.27	8.37	9.53	10.74	11.97
20	7.07	8.19	9.37	10.59	11.84

Table 7-4 Percent Withdrawals and Years to Depletion

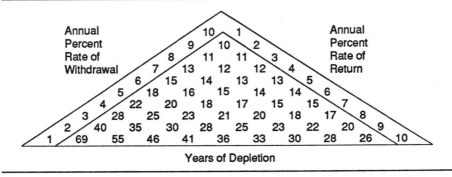

Assume, for example, that you are considering the withdrawal of 10 percent from your investment each year, and you believe that the investment can appreciate on average about seven percent each year. At the intersection of these two percentages is the number 17. This means you can expect your investment to last for 17 years. Of course you would not want to assume that this number is cast in stone. As time passes and interest rate projections change, you would want to re-enter the table to get a new forecast. The table can also be used in other ways. For example, if you wanted your money to last for 30 years and you thought you could earn seven percent on the investment, then you could withdraw eight percent a year.

Still another way to calculate long-term withdrawals is to use your life expectancy for the withdrawal period. If you wish to obtain a lifetime income from your investment, this approach makes sense. To determine an annual amount so that you never run out, simply divide the current investment balance by your life expectancy in years. As both your life expectancy and investment balance will change each year, the withdrawal amount will also change annually. Table 7-5 provides the IRS life expectancy table used for determining minimum annual withdrawals from an Individual Retirement Account. It can be used for calculating withdrawals from any investment.

As an example, suppose you have a European mutual fund with a value of $110,000. Moreover, assume that you are 64 years old and wish to start the dollar averaging withdrawal process. From the table you can see that your life expectancy is 20.8 years. The withdrawal for the current year would be $110,000/20.8, or $5,288.46. Let us further suppose that during the year the fund's value appreciated, so despite your withdrawal, the fund was worth $112,000 at the end of the year. Your life expectancy at the end of the next year is 20.0 (From Table 7-5, age 65). Your withdrawal for the following year would therefore be $112,000/20.0, or $5,600. If we further assume for the sake of illustration that your fund declined instead of increased and your balance was $107,000, your withdrawal would then be $107,000/20.0, or $5,350. As you can imagine, the withdrawal amounts with this system will vary from year to year. You can be sure, however, that you will never run out of money using this method, no matter how long you live.

Table 7-5 IRS Life Expectancy Table

Age	Divisor	Age	Divisor
55	28.6	86	6.5
56	27.7	87	6.1
57	26.8	88	5.7
58	25.9	89	5.3
59	25.0	90	5.0
60	24.2	91	4.7
61	23.3	92	4.4
62	22.5	93	4.1
63	21.6	94	3.9
64	20.8	95	3.7
65	20.0	96	3.4
66	19.2	97	3.2
67	18.4	98	3.0
68	17.6	99	2.8
69	16.8	100	2.7
70	16.0	101	2.5
71	15.3	102	2.3
72	14.6	103	2.1
73	13.9	104	1.9
74	13.2	105	1.8
75	12.5	106	1.6
76	11.9	107	1.4
77	11.2	108	1.3
78	10.6	109	1.1
79	10.0	110	1.0
80	9.5	111	.9
81	8.9	112	.8
82	8.4	113	.7
83	7.9	114	.6
84	7.4	115	.5
85	6.9		

Source: IRS Tax Information Publications, Volume 4, 1989, p.311.

REFERENCES

Dorf, Richard, *The New Mutual Fund Investment Advisor* (Chicago, IL: Probus Publishing, 1986).

IRS Tax Information Publications Volume 4, 1989, p. 311.

Lichello, Robert, *How To Make $1,000,000 in the Stock Market Automatically* (New York, NY: Signet, 1985).

Sherman, Michael, *The Retirement Account Calculator* (Chicago, IL: Contemporary Books, Inc., 1986).

Willis, Clint, "Beyond Dollar-Cost Averaging," *Money*, July, 1988, pp. 105-109.

CHAPTER 8

Asset Allocation Strategies

Beginning in the 1970's several money managers and investment writers began to concentrate on the concept of *asset allocation* for achieving investment objectives. The basic idea is to spread or allocate your money within specified categories of investments. There were some mutual funds established whose entire investment strategy is based on this philosophy. This investment approach can be divided into two categories—*permanent allocation strategies* and *variable allocation strategies*. Both of these strategies work well with the dollar averaging techniques discussed in chapter seven. We will look first at the easiest one to implement, permanent allocation strategies.

PERMANENT ALLOCATION STRATEGIES

The term "permanent" is used because your allocations to chosen investment categories do not change because of any economic or market conditions. We never change allocations because of what we think will happen to the stock market, interest rates, inflation or other factors. Permanent allocation strategies can be *equal* or *investor selected*.

Equal Allocation Strategy

Equal allocation is the first of our permanent allocation strategies. This strategy is simple to understand and simple to implement. *It can literally be implemented in 30 minutes a year!* This strategy is spelled out in detail in one of the best investment books of the 1980's, *Why the Best-Laid Investment Plans Usually Go Wrong,* by Harry Browne.

While we do not agree with all the conclusions of the book (for example, we are not as optimistic about gold as a long-term investment), we believe Browne has done a very fine job of analyzing the contemporary economic and investment environment and pointing out the shortcomings of many of the current "get rich quick" investment strategies. An investor interested in the underlying philosophy behind this strategy can learn more about it by reading Browne's entire book.

His strategy is a simple one. He recommends dividing one's in vestment money equally among four different kinds of investments:

25% in common stocks
25% in government bonds
25% in cash and cash equivalents
25% in gold

Once each year the investor shifts investments among the four to adjust them so that each category again equals 25 percent of the total amount invested. New investments that are made during the course of the year are allocated to the four categories on a 25 percent basis.

The idea behind this approach that allows it to work is that different investments do well at different times. Common stocks performed less well than other investments in the early to mid-1970's, but they did better than most other investments in the 1980's. Gold did very well in the late 1970's and early 1980's, but it has trailed most other investments since. This approach is designed to take profits from investments which have done well and move them into other investments when their prices are low. To illustrate, when gold prices are rising and stock prices are lagging, the process of getting each investment back to 25 percent would involve selling some gold and using the money to buy stocks at a very good time, i.e. when stock prices are relatively low. Browne says his research indicates that this approach, if applied over the 17 years prior to publication of his book, would have provided an annual compound investment return of 12 percent.

The equal allocation strategy can by used by internationally oriented investors by changing the mix of investments to reflect a world-view. As an example, the following no-load (commision-free) mutual funds could be used to achieve this objective.

Scudder Global Equities Fund
T. Rowe Price International Bond Fund
Dreyfus World-Wide Dollar Money Market Fund
Financial Strategic Portfolio—Gold

Implementation of the permanent portfolio approach is very simple. You need take just two steps:

Step 1: Establish your initial allocations so that they are distributed equally across the four categories of investments, and make additional (for example, monthly) investments in the same twenty-five percent proportions. Using the international funds just mentioned, your investments would look like the following for a $50,000 portfolio:

Amount	*Investment*
$12,500	Scudder Global Equities Fund
$12,500	T. Rowe Price International Bond Fund
$12,500	Dreyfus World-Wide Dollar Money Market
$12,500	Financial Strategic Portfolio—Gold

If each month you had an additional $1000 to invest, you would send $250 to each of the four mutual funds listed.

Step 2: Once each year, calculate what you need to do to get your allocations back to 25 percent in each account. Then call the mutual fund companies to adjust your accounts so that each of them once again contains about 25 percent of your funds. It is not important when you do this so long as you do it at the same time each year.

As an example, let us assume that your year-ending statement shows your accumulation balances to be:

Scudder Global Equities Fund	$16,000
T. Rowe Price International Bond Fund	$11,000
Dreyfus World-Wide Dollar MM Fund	$18,000
Financial Strategic Portfolio—Gold	$15,000
	$60,000

You want $15,000 (25 percent) in each account, so you can leave your Gold Fund alone since it contains this amount already. To balance your other accounts you will need to:

1. Sell $3000 of your Dreyfus World-Wide Dollar Money Market fund and send the proceeds to the T. Rowe Price International Bond Fund.
2. Sell $1000 of your Scudder Global Equities Fund and send the proceeds to the T. Rowe Price International Bond Fund.

This will restore each account to the 25 percent level, and you will have nothing more to do for another year. With the use of a hand calculator, this process should take no more than 30 minutes a year.

The advantage of using no-load mutual funds for this strategy is obvious. It is easy to make the year-end adjustments at no cost and periodic new investments during the year can be made without paying a commission charge.

This approach does require one very important personal quality—*self-discipline*, as it requires you to take action against the trends. At precisely the time you are reading in the newspapers and hearing talk at cocktail parties about how a particular type of investment is going down, your strategy tells you to invest more of your retirement money in that investment. This can be psychologically difficult to do. Moreover, if you are the type who gets frustrated because your investment strategy does not seem to produce quick results, forget this approach. If you can discipline yourself to stick with the strategy for the long pull, but you want to spend very little time on money matters, this may be just the approach for you.

Investor Selected Allocation Strategy

This strategy is exactly like the one just described except that instead of investments receiving equal allocations, the allocations are selected by the investor based on his or her personal situation and investment objectives. It is not necessary to use four funds; either fewer or more might better meet a particular investor's needs.

We can look at several alternative applications of this strategy. There may be an ultra conservative investor who wants to take advantage of this approach but with minimal risk. An appropriate portfolio for that person might be:

40% to Dreyfus World Wide Money Market fund
30% to T. Rowe Price International Bond Fund
20% to Vanguard World, International Growth Fund
10% to Financial Strategic Portfolio—Gold

The portfolio is conservative in several ways. Dreyfus World Wide Money Market Fund, offering a virtually risk-free return, comprises 40 percent of the total. Another 30 percent is in a bond fund, which will fluctuate in price as interest rates change, but should still be less volatile over the long run than that expected from equity funds. The Vanguard World fund is a conservative equity fund with a low Beta (less volatile than the U.S. stock market). Finally, the Gold portfolio comprises only 10 percent of the total.

An alternative to this approach which would still provide a conservative, low risk portfolio might be accomplished using only three funds:

40% to Dreyfus World Wide Dollar Money Market Fund
30% to T. Rowe Price International Bond Fund
30% to Vanguard World International Equities Fund

Another investor may have a higher risk tolerance and want a more aggressive portfolio, with more volatility. An appropriate mix of funds could be:

40% to Scudder Global Equities Fund
30% to T. Rowe Price International Bond Fund
20% to Financial Strategic Portfolio—Gold
10% to Dreyfus World Wide Dollar Money Market Fund

As before, if additional investments are made, the new money is allocated in the proportion specified by the allocation mix.

Another alternative would be what might be called an *age related strategy*. This would involve an allocation that is designed to be adjusted and reduce risk about once a decade as the investor grows older. It would look something like the numbers shown in Table 8-1.

Table 8-1 Percentages For Monthly Allocation and Accumulation Balances

	Age 25	Age 35	Age 45	Age 55
Scudder Global Equities	50%	45%	40%	35%
T. Rowe Price Int. Bond	35%	30%	25%	20%
Financial Strategic Gold	15%	15%	10%	10%
Dreyfus World M M. Fund		10%	25%	35%

As the table shows, with increasing age the proportion of total investments becomes more conservative. You can, of course, adjust the percentages to suit yourself and even use different funds if you prefer. All of the plans described would be implemented in the same two-step procedure; 1) set the initial investments and periodic additional allocations on the basis of the preferred percentages, and 2) once each year make the necessary adjustments in the accumulation balances to bring them back into line with those percentages.

VARIABLE ALLOCATION STRATEGIES

Variable allocation strategies are similar to permanent allocation strategies, but they differ in two important ways. First, with variable allocation strategies the percentage distribution for the initial investments and the additional investment allocations need not be the same. Second, and this is why they are called *variable*, with variable allocation strategies the additional investment allocations (or total investment accumulations) may vary based on *external economic factors* rather than on the preferences of the investor.

This approach will involve somewhat more time than those described above. It will be necessary for the investor to set aside perhaps 15 minutes or so a week to check the markets and whatever economic indicators are being used.

The goal of variable allocation strategies is to be more heavily invested in stocks (equity funds) when economic factors are favorable and mainly in other investments when conditions affecting stocks are unfavorable. Such strategies often use interest rates as an indicator of when to be invested in equities on the assumption that equities usually move in an inverse relationship with interest rates.

Interest Rate Strategy

One such approach is recommended by William E. Donoghue, who has probably done more research on money market funds than anyone else in the investment field. In his book, *No-Load Mutual Fund Guide*, he presents what he calls his "12 percent solution." This involves switching between a money market fund and a stock fund based on the interest rate yield of money market funds, as follows:

Invested in Money Market Fund	Money Market Funds Yield	Invested in Equity Fund
100%	13%	0%
75%	12%	25%
50%	11%	50%
25%	10%	75%
0%	9%	100%

Donoghue says you should be 100 percent invested in money market funds if they are paying 13 percent or more. When the rates fall to 12 percent you should begin to move a portion of your funds into stock funds. Donoghue was writing in the early 1980's when U.S. interest rates were very high. Someone using his approach today for U.S. stocks would have to adjust the figures in the center column down by two or three points to reflect the generally lower rate environment. For international equity investments, the figures given can be used as is, assuming the mutual fund used has investments diversified across many countries around the world. If investments are made in a mutual fund that is concentrating its investments in a single country or single region of the world, the center figures would have to be adjusted to reflect the interest rate situation typical to the target area.

As an example, if an investor were to invest in the European Economic Community in the early 1990's using a no-load mutual fund (for example, the Financial Strategic European Fund), the following table illustrates how the Donoghue approach could be modified to fit this situation.

Proportion of Transferable Investment Invested in Money Market Fund	Money Market Funds Yield	Proportion of Transferable Investment Invested In Equity Fund
80%	10%	20%
60%	9%	40%
40%	8%	60%
20%	7%	80%

The center column has lower percentages than that shown in the previous table, reflecting the range of yields thought to be normal for this area. Another change is with the range of percentages given. We believe strongly in diversification and in the principle that one should not have all of his or her investment money in one place. Therefore, this chart does not use the 100 percent figure. It never has more than 80 percent in either the equity or the money market fund. An investment strategy using this chart could be implemented in the following way:

Step 1: Choose an equity mutual fund and use it in conjunction with a money market fund which permits free switching by telephone.

Step 2: Invest 50 percent of your funds allocated to this strategy in the equity fund and the other 50 percent in the money market fund. For any later investments plan so that 50 percent of the new contributions will go into each of the funds. *Then leave this 50-50 invest-*

ment allocation plan for additional funds alone. Don't attempt to adjust it each time you change your investment accumulation balances. To get started, let your funds accumulate with 50 percent in each account until a change in money market yield calls for a change in the accumulation percentages.

Step 3: Use a chart similar to the one above, or alter it to satisfy yourself. Based on this chart, you will be 80 percent invested in the money market fund whenever it is yielding more than 10 percent and only 20 percent invested in that fund when it is yielding less than seven percent.

Step 4: Once each week check the current yield of the money market fund. This can be accomplished through a telephone call (most mutual fund companies have 24 hour automated systems for obtaining quotes), or by checking a financial newspaper like *Barron's.* As the yield on the money market fund changes to the next significant "whole number," adjust your accumulations balances based on your chart. You will find that you will not be making frequent changes. Interest rates usually do not fluctuate so rapidly as to cause you to make more than a few such transfers a yeaı

Why, you may ask, do we recommend shifting the accumulation balances but not the additional investment allocations in this plan? We want to keep the plan simple to implement while protecting your funds. Using this approach, the shift of accumulation balances will protect the money you have invested in the equity fund from major loss while at the same time providing that any new money you are investing will take advantage of the current price declines.

An additional advantage of this approach is its "do-it-yourself" nature. You can adjust the numbers in the chart and the frequency of adjustment to suit yourself. If you prefer to check with money market rates monthly rather than weekly, the plan will still work. Donoghue says his "12 percent solution" would have yielded an average compound rate of 19.1 percent in the years from 1975 (when money market funds were a very new idea) to the time of the publication of his book, a figure considerably above what would be expected from a "buy, hold and try to forget it" approach.

Trend Reversal Strategies

Martin Zweig suggests another way to use variable allocation strategies. He takes a very systematic, research oriented approach to his investment analysis. In his book, *Winning With New IRA's*, Zweig says a four percent reversal in direction is likely to indicate a major trend shift for stock and bond funds. Although it takes a little more time than the plans outlined above, this approach can be easily applied to global mutual funds.

Our variation of the four percent reversal strategy, would be as follows. If a fund has moved gradually, week by week, to a price of $10 and then falls to $9.60, that would represent a four percent decline. It would then be time to sell the fund. The change need not occur all at once. If a fund reaches a price level of $10, then drops over several weeks to $9.90, $9.85, $9.75 and $9.60, when it reaches $9.60 that represents a four percent decline from the high. That would be the sell signal. The same principle would apply when prices start back up.

When a fund rises four percent above its recent low, that becomes a buy signal. You can use the trend reversal strategy in the following manner:

Step 1: Choose two or three global equity funds to use along with a money market fund, bond fund, gold fund and other investments that meet your asset allocation objectives.

Step 2: Choose a set of percentages so as to distribute your initial investment and subsequent investments rather evenly among the two or three chosen funds. As an example, you might want to have 40 percent of your equity investments going into the most conservative of your three funds and 30 percent into each of the other two.

Step 3: Once a week check the closing price of each of your equity funds. Keep a written record of the weekly closing prices of each fund so that you can identify when a four percent trend reversal has occurred.

Step 4: When an equity fund falls four percent, shift the accumulation (but not the additional investment of new funds) into the money market fund. Our philosophy here is the same as for the interest rate strategy. Shifting the accumulation protects the money you have already invested. Leaving the new investment allocation percentage alone enables your new money to take advantage of the current lower prices, a dollar averaging strategy.

Step 5: When an equity fund which has been falling in price reverses direction and rises four percent, shift a portion of the money in the money market fund back into that fund. You will probably want to invest an amount in the fund which about equals the amount you shifted out of that fund the last time you moved into the money market fund.

Remember, so long as the price is moving in the same direction without a four percent price reversal, leave your investments alone. This way you will profit when the long term price trend of your equity funds is rising, and when the trend is downward, your money will be sitting safely in the Money Market Fund. Zweig says his four percent model (only slightly different from our approach) would have provided an average annual return of 18.9 percent if used on U.S. stocks between 1966 and 1985.

Table 8-2 shows an example of what a no-load mutual fund portfolio using this variable allocation strategy might look like before and after a four-percent sell signal (to simplify the table, it is assumed that no dollar changes took place in any of the funds from the initial purchase to the time of the sell signal). Both equity funds initially had $5,000 invested in them and the money market fund was uninvested. When the Vanguard World-International fund reversed by 4 percent from its recent high point, the entire proceeds of the fund were sold and the money was moved to the Dreyfus World Dollar Money Market fund. The equity fund portion of the entire portfolio dropped by 50 percent (58 percent equity exposure to 29 percent equity) as the only remaining equity mutual fund is the Scudder Global Equities fund. If the Scudder fund later reversed by 4 percent to the downside, it too would be sold, reducing stock market exposure to zero. Remember that, even if you have "switched out" of one or both of the equity funds, any new money that you invest will be invested with the *original proportions* as shown at the top of Table 8-2. This is to allow dollar averaging to come into play by buying new shares at lower prices.

Table 8-2 Portfolio Changes Resulting from a 4 Percent Reversal

Starting Portfolio	Dollars	Approximate Percentage
Equity Funds		
Vanguard World-Int.	$10,000	29%
Scudder Global Equities	$10,000	29%
Money Market Fund:		
Dreyfus World Wide Dollar	$0	0%
Bond Fund:		
T. Rowe Price Int. Bond	$10,000	29%
Gold Fund:		
Financial Strategic Gold	$5,000	14%

Portfolio After 4% Reversal (Sell) of Vanguard World-Int.

Equity Funds:		
Vanguard World-Int.	$0	0%
Scudder Global Equities	$10,000	29%
Bond Fund:		
T. Rowe Price Int. Bond	$10,000	29%
Gold Fund:		
Financial Strategic Gold	$1,000	14%

If you decide the four percent reversal approach causes you to make more switches that you like, you can adjust and use a five percent, six percent or other figure for your reversal number. This will cause you to make fewer switches, but it will also reduce your return somewhat as you catch each trend reversal somewhat later in the reversal process. This approach, like those previously mentioned, has the advantage of allowing you to adjust it to meet your own needs and preferences.

REFERENCES

Browne, Harry, *The Economic Time Bomb* (New York, NY: St. Martin's Press, 1989).

Browne, Harry, *Why the Best-Laid Investment Plans Usually Go Wrong* (New York, NY: William Morrow, 1987).

Donoghue, William E., with Thomas Tilling, *No-Load Mutual Fund Guide* (New York, NY: Harper and Row, 1983).

Donoghue, William E., with Robert Chapman Wood, *The Donoghue Strategies* (New York, NY: Bantam Books, 1989).

Hirsch, Yale, *Don't Sell Stocks on Monday* (New York, NY: Facts on File Publications, 1986).

Merriman, Paul A., and Dowd, Merle E., *Market Timing with No-Load Mutual Funds* (New York, NY: Henry Holt and Co., 1986).

Zweig, Martin, *Winning with New IRA's* (New York, NY: Warner, 1987).

CHAPTER 9

Timing Models for International Securities

In Chapter Seven we discussed the concept of dollar averaging as an approach for avoiding the worry of up and down market movements. As you remember, this system works best when a long investing horizon is available and there is not a time in the future when all the funds may suddenly be required for use. Money is eased into the investments over time during the investing years and eased out during the take-out years. With this method, the price level of the investment at any given point in time has very little bearing on the overall performance of the dollar averaging investment system.

The concept of asset allocation was introduced in Chapter Eight, which provided a broad framework within which the dollar averaging approach could be used. Diversification across many investment vehicles was the key to achieving risk reduction and consistency of overall performance. In this chapter we discuss timing models. These models are especially useful for investors who want to assume greater risk and wish to be more active in the management of their investments in the hope of obtaining greater returns. Moreover, for those investors who may need to remove all of their investment money quickly and without the luxury of advance notice, the timing model approach can reduce the chance of a large loss at the time the money is needed.

While this chapter discusses the timing of securities, you should avoid the temptation to make short term in-and-out trades in the international arena. It is better to attempt to catch major up-moves and avoid the major down-moves than attempt to profit from every wiggle in securities prices. Not only is it difficult if not impossible to catch all the minor movements but the commission charges on the constant trading will eat deeply into any profits generated. The basic timing approach discussed here is to attempt to ride the major up-movements that last from months to years while avoiding significant losses of capital from a major down trend. To achieve these objectives, both economic models and technical models are discussed.

ECONOMIC MODELING

Knowledge of the economic business cycle of a country can be extremely useful as a model to time the purchases and sales of investments. As various investment options tend to perform differently during different stages of the business cycle, this knowledge provides the key to knowing which investments will do best as economic conditions change. Figure 9-1 shows how a typical business cycle behaves. Instead of growing smoothly, economies tend to go through periods of expansion and contraction. These expansion-contraction cycles are known as business or economic cycles of a country.

As the figure shows, the expansionary phase of the cycle eventually runs out of steam and a contraction in business activity takes place. Early on, the contraction simply means a reduction in rate of positive growth. A growth rate of four percent, for example, may be reduced to three percent. If the contraction persists over time, the rate of growth can turn negative (for example, a growth rate of *minus* two percent). When the growth rate becomes negative, the term "recession" is used. Eventually, the downturn leads to another expansion as the economy begins growing again.

Figure 9-1 The Repeating Business Cycle

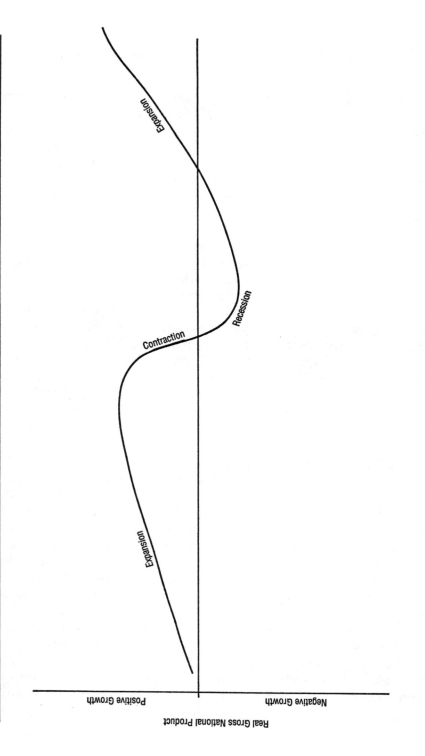

How do these expansion-contraction cycles arise? As an economy grows, more and more labor and productive capacity is put to use. The increased employment means more money is available for spending, which in turn results in an increase in demand for goods and services. During this phase, manufacturing businesses increase production to meet both current and projected demand, and services expand for the same reason by hiring more personnel and opening more outlets.

As the expansion continues, several factors begin to operate which will eventually kill the expansion. As business profits increase, more and more money is available for investing. This money flows into real estate, securities markets, expansion of existing business facilities, and into new business ventures. Moreover, the easy availability of investment money and strong operating cash flow encourages the purchase and consolidation of existing companies, often with borrowed money, which is readily available. As these events continue and the economic expansion matures, inflation begins to increase. The abundance of investment money moving to real estate, security markets and other assets bids up prices. Further business expansion becomes difficult without a significant increase in operating costs. Skilled labor becomes nearly impossible to obtain without offering higher pay, and overtime wages may have to be paid to get additional production out of existing resources. Accompanying this general price rise is an over-capacity of both production and services, which is created based on overly optimistic projections of future demand. Attendant with this over-capacity is an excess of inventory which accumulates during the expansionary period. This inventory exists in terms of finished production goods, housing, business buildings, productive facilities, and employees on the payroll. Moreover, many companies find themselves with large debt loads from heavy borrowing during the optimistic expansionary period.

It is these excesses, along with the attendant rise in prices, that sets the stage for an economic downturn. The government, through the banking system, attempts to "calm" the economic expansion through a boost in short-term interest rates. Higher short-term rates have the effect of eventually slowing the economic expansion, thereby reducing the rate of inflation. The slowing takes place because businesses (and consumers) find it more difficult to borrow money at the higher interest rates. As interest rates represent the cost of renting money, higher rates mean greater business costs and therefore less money left over in profits for the borrower. For the consumer, higher rates means greater difficulty in qualifying for loans and less money left for discretionary purchases after making loan payments. As demand for goods and services drops off, a net reduction in employment may occur as businesses move to cut costs. Price rises tend to moderate as the reduction in demand faces an abundance of goods and services. Eventually the expansionary part of the business cycle is choked off and an economic downturn begins.

Ideally, the overheated economy will slow down, reduce inflationary pressures, then go on to another expansionary phase. In practice, however, this "soft landing" rarely occurs. Instead, the engineered slowdown becomes a mild-to-severe recession, where the rate of growth becomes negative. The recessionary period brings much economic pain and wrings the excesses out of the economy through bankruptcies, layoffs, and inventory mark-downs. This tough period establishes the foundation for lower rates of interest, moderate price increases and a new expansion.

This cycle of expansion followed by contraction repeats itself over and over again throughout the world in market economies, so it can be used as a basic framework for making investment decisions. Figure 9-2 illustrates how the cycle relates to the basic four investment types of: 1) stocks; 2) bonds; 3) money market funds; and 4) inflation sensitive instruments.

Stocks

Stocks tend to do well during the period that extends from just before the start of the expansionary period to just before the start of the contraction period. Before the expansionary period begins, investors look ahead to better times and start to accumulate stocks. As the market firms, optimism begins to return to the equity investors, attracting additional investment money. As the economy revives and profits begin to rebound, the market becomes even more attractive. The party for stocks is not over until interest rates begin

Figure 9-2 The Repeating Business Cycle and Favorable Investment Periods

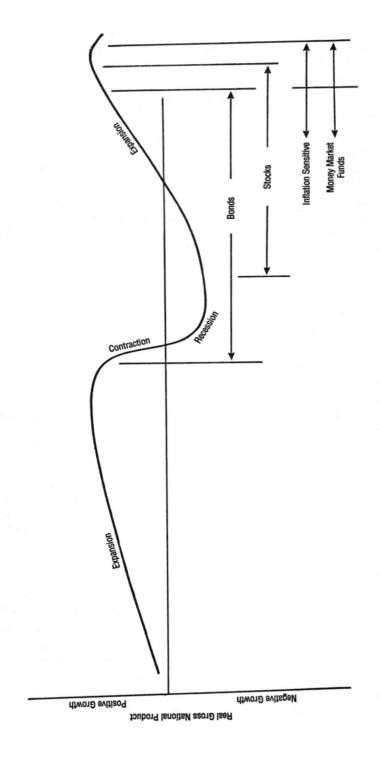

rising late in the expansion phase. Investors then look ahead at the negative effect these rates will have on corporate profits, and think about the high yields that can be obtained with no risk using money market funds. As the future for stocks looks less and less attractive, selling hits the equity markets, ending the favorable phase until the cycle repeats itself again.

The stock cycle can be analyzed in further detail by assessing the types of stock investments that provide the greatest return throughout the favorable equity investment period. Richard A. Stoken, in his book *Strategic Investment Timing* (Probus Publishing, 1990) analyzed this favorable period and divided it into three phases. He found that by selecting the right type of stock investment during each of the three phases within the favorable period, a much larger gain can be achieved than by simply buying and holding stocks throughout the period. Although his work referenced the U.S. domestic market exclusively, the basic approach applies to markets everywhere.

The first phase is the recovery period, when the market initially rebounds from oversold bear market levels. During this period the market rise is indiscriminate and most all stocks go up in value. Stock-picking is not all that important during this phase, as the rising tide of equity investing "lifts all boats." In the second or middle phase, a transion period exists where investors become more selective. The focus for investing is on companies showing earnings growth, so they tend to perform the best. These companies are typically those that are large and well established. The third or mature phase marks the period in the economic expansion where capital goods spending surges. During this phase the large companies will have already been bid up in price to reflect most all of the earnings to be expected in the current expansionary cycle. Investors shift their emphasis to the "undiscovered" smaller companies whose prices have not yet been bid up by investment demand. Figure 9-3 illustrates these stages on the business cycle, with the figure reflecting international investing options.

Early in the favorable period for stocks, country mutual funds are shown as the recommended international equity vehicle. Since all stocks tend to do well at the start of a cyclic bull market, the use of mutual funds, with their built-in diversification, will provide an excellent opportunity for appreciation without individual stock risk.

Figure 9-3 Idealized Equity Investments During the Favorable Stock Periods

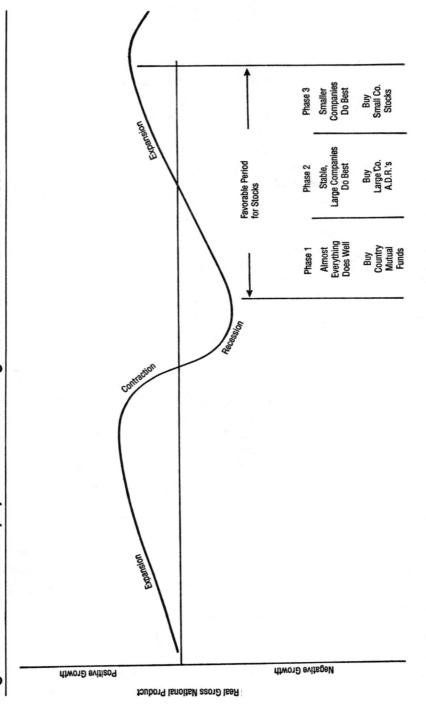

The discount that closed-end funds have at this time will likely be reduced during the price run-up, thereby increasing the return for investors using this vehicle. During phase two, when the bulk of investors are more selective, large company ADR's (or a mutual fund that concentrates on these large and highly profitable companies) will tend to do best. Late in the business expansion (phase three), a shift to smaller company investments tends to do best. This means the purchase of smaller company ADR's or smaller company stocks traded on foreign exchanges are preferred. Unfortunately, this late stage equity preference may be difficult to incorporate on an international basis because small company ADR's may not be available. Moreover, foreign regulations may make the direct purchase of stocks difficult, and lack of obtainable information about these companies can compound your problems in choosing a specific investment. For these cases, phase two stocks will have to be held until the favorable period for stocks is over.

Bonds

Bonds tend to perform best from the point when the contraction is well under way (interest rates have peaked and are about to fall) to the point in the expansionary period where inflation has begun to heat up. Once the economic contraction is established, inflation tends to moderate as demand for goods is reduced. Short-term interest rates are lowered by the central bank in an effort to get the economy growing again. Long rates follow as inflation continues to moderate. Because bond prices move inversely to interest rates, bonds move higher. Bonds tend to be favorable investments until interest rates start to advance, which typically happens near the end of the expansionary phase when inflation begins heating up.

Inflation Sensitive Instruments

Inflation sensitive instruments typically rise in value near the end of the expansionary period and well into the contraction phase. This is because the expansionary phase brings with it the demand excesses that push up prices. This favorable phase lasts until the contraction phase begins, when the supply of goods and services is greater than the demand, which has been crippled by the slowdown. Money market funds also are attractive as investments during the high inflation periods. This is because, once the inflation period is underway, interest rates rise to cover the declining value of money, and other financial investments (stocks and bonds) are competitively unfavorable. At other times, money market funds offer safety but comparatively low yields.

Special Factors Affecting the Business Cycle

Each business cycle in a country tends to be unique in one way or another. Often there are factors that may affect the "normal" course of cyclic events just described. For example, the shape of the cycle can change, with a shorter than expected expansion rapidly turning into a recession, or a long expansion followed by a low-growth period but no recession. The relationship between the business cycle and types of investments that are in bull and bear markets can also change. Factors that may produce anomalies are many. Some can be predicted and tracked, others arise suddenly and can only be reacted to by the investor. The basic economic stability that many North Americans have enjoyed in the past cannot be assumed to exist in the future global marketplace. The following set of potentially disruptive factors should be kept in mind by all business cycle watchers.

Political Considerations. Political instability can have terrible effects on securities markets. Markets abhor uncertainty, so no matter what phase of an economic cycle a country may be in, if an unstable political situation exists, financial markets may not respond normally to the current economic situation. Most countries have some political parties with socialist leanings that are viewed negatively by business and investors. Elections in which these parties gain influence can have a negative effect on markets and the economy. In addition, foreign investors may become more cautious on making new investments and a net outflow of money from the markets may result. Moreover, history has shown that elected representatives love to tinker with the fortunes of their citizens through legislative action, much of it oriented toward quick-fix solutions rather than focused on building a stronger economic structure. For example, legislation that "bails out" companies in bankruptcy at the taxpayers expense may slow the economy and cause interest rates to rise, thereby prolonging a recession. Also, any legislation that leads to a weakening of the currency may have the undesired effects of increasing inflation (the cost of imported goods rise as the currency drops), and decreasing the amount of foreign investment in the country. For many laws that are passed, one may not know what the effect may be on security prices or the economic cycle. The uncertainty alone, however, may well damage the financial markets.

Foreign Energy Dependency. The greater a country's energy dependency, the greater the risk of a disruption in the business cycle by events beyond their control. The Middle East is an area where vast numbers of people live in poverty, yet a comparatively few live in immense wealth. These conditions tend to be inherently unstable over the long run. If one adds to this basic instability religious fervor and non-democratic institutions, oil supply disruptions are to be expected, with only their frequency, timing and ultimate effect on a dependent country's business cycle open to question.

Debt. Large external foreign interest payments by a country can result in a forced slow-growth scenario for an economy over a long period of time as the interest payments eat up funds that could be used for economic stimulation. Similarly, a large budget deficit makes economic stimulation during periods of economic slowdown more difficult to achieve, thereby prolonging an economic down turn. Moreover, the need to sell bonds to raise public funds to finance a deficit can keep interest rates high (to attract the needed funds), further suppressing economic growth.

Sudden Natural Disasters. Earthquakes, floods, storms, droughts and diseases all carry the potential to greatly affect a country's economic situation and securities markets. While these disasters usually cannot be predicted, degree of preparation for them can often be assessed, along with the susceptibility of the economic infrastructure to their damaging effects.

Sudden Man-Made Disasters. An unexpected entry into an armed conflict can rapidly modify the economic prospects for a country.

Fortunately, the easing of global tensions makes a major war among superpowers in the foreseeable future extremely unlikely. Smaller regional conflicts are always a possibility, however, with the negative effect of such conflicts magnified by the proliferation of nuclear weapons. Besides armed conflicts, the possibility of nuclear and chemical accidents, with their potentially disastrous economic effects should be recognized.

The key to using the economic cycle as a model for making international investments is to identify the current phase of the country's cycle, while also assessing the prospects for a disruption in the normal course of events. To successfully accomplish this feat involves tracking relevant economic indicators while constantly keeping up with international news. To assess the economic cycle, this means knowing the status of: 1) the economic growth rate (GNP); 2) the inflation rate trend; and 3) the interest rate trend. By relating the state of these indicators to the business cycle description provided earlier in this chapter, you will know when the various investment options are in their favorable or unfavorable phases. To guard against a large drawdown in your account from unexpected events or other factors that might disrupt the normal pattern of the business cycle, diversification should be established.

As we indicated in chapter three, splitting up your investment money into parts and investing in many different ways should be a cornerstone of your investment strategy. As such, if a disaster should befall any one of your investments, your aggregate performance will not be affected to a major degree. The more susceptible a country or region of the world is to unexpected events, the more important it is for your money to be dispersed to other places.

TECHNICAL MODELS

Technical analysis provides an alternative approach for deciding when to invest in stocks, bonds, money market funds and inflation sensitive investments. Its use is based on the assumption that clues to future price movements of a financial instrument can be found by looking at its past and present behavior. To accomplish this task, historical price and volume data are represented in graphical forms and are both analyzed and mathematically manipulated in a myriad of ways. Specifically, technical analysis uses this data to assess trends and trend reversals, excesses in price movements, and divergences between important indicators. Each of these provides its own perspective on the status of the financial instrument in question. The basic idea behind the technical model is to weigh the totality of evidence from these technical indicators and take action when the weight of evidence indicates a buy or a sell.

Because of its mathematical nature, technical analysis was once an approach used only by those well versed in scientific analysis. However, in recent years this has changed with the advent of microcomputers and inexpensive technical analysis software. Now quite sophisticated mathematical methods are available for use by anyone who has an interest in the approach and access to a computer. In this chapter we will assume that a computer is available for making calculations and graphing the data, so mathematical formulas and explanations will not be provided. Table 9-1 provides a list of major technical software packages that are available to the individual investor. For a more comprehensive list, the *Individual Investor's Guide to Computerized Investing,* published annually by the American Association of Individual Investors (625 North Michigan Avenue, Chicago, IL 60611), is a very useful source. Other more current sources include the advertisements in *Investor's Daily* and *Barron's.* Demonstration disks are usually available for analysis software at low or no cost, providing an opportunity to use the software first-hand before buying. They can be obtained by calling or writing to the addresses given in Table 9-1.

Trends and Trend Reversals

"The trend is your friend" is one of the oldest sayings in investment management. Price trends tend to persist over time, giving investors the chance to ride with the movement and prepare themselves for opportunities that arise when the trend changes.

Table 9-1 Major Technical Analysis Software

Compu Trac	Compu Trac Software, Inc. 1017 Pleasant Street New Orleans, LA 70115 (504) 895-1474
Dow Jones Market Analyzer Plus	Dow Jones & Company, Inc. P.O. Box 300 Princeton, NJ 08543-0300 (609) 520-4641
Fund Master T	FundVest Inc. 337 Boston Road Billerca, MA 01821-9975 (508) 663-3330
Metastock-Professional	Equis International P.O. Box 26743 Salt Lake City, UT 84126 (800) 882-3040
Stockpak II	Standard & Poor's Corp. 26 Broadway New York, NY 10004 (212) 208-8581
Telescan Analyzer	Telescan, Inc. 2900 Wilcrest, Suite 400 Houston, TX 77042 (800) 727-952-1060

One of the simplest and most commonly used means of assessing a trend is to look at a graph of prices in an effort to find trend clues. While up-to-date published graphs of international equity market averages are readily available, you will have trouble finding up-to-date published graphs of most anything else on the international scene. For graphs of individual stocks, non-equity securities and mutual funds, plan to create them yourself using computerized technical analysis software.

One way to determine a trend from looking at a price history is to assess the pattern of high and low movements. A rising trend is characterized by higher highs and higher lows. A falling trend is characterized by lower highs and lower lows. Figure 9-4 shows how this assessment is made.

As long as the pattern displays the higher high higher-low pattern, the up-trend is assumed to be intact and investments can be made on this basis. When the opposing pattern is seen, the investor would stay away from making commitments.

When the trend ends, the patterns traced by the price movements are interrupted. Instead of the expected high-low relationships, the price pattern typically traces a "W" pattern for a market bottom, and an "M" pattern for a market top. These patterns are very important to students of technical analysis as they signal an end to the higher-highs and lower-lows pattern that characterized the previous trend.

Unfortunately, the patterns that are seen on a chart are not always clear cut. It is usually easier to identify the trends after they have occurred than while they are occurring. This is a weakness of this approach and it has encouraged the development of other trend-defining approaches.

Another common method for assessing trends that is somewhat less ambiguous is to use the trend line approach. When prices are rising, a trend line can be established by connecting the low points of the rising prices, when prices are falling, a trend line can be connected between the falling price peaks. Figure 9-5 illustrates this approach.

In practice, trend lines should be drawn "thickly," since the inherent randomness in short-term price change movement makes a precise increase or decrease along a line unlikely.

A final method for assessing price trends is to use a moving average technique. A moving average is a set of data points, each point of which is found by taking an average of historical prices. For each period's new price data, a new moving average data value is calculated. Figure 9-6 shows a 40 week moving average superimposed on prices for the Financial Programs European mutual fund. As

Figure 9-4 Trend Determination and Patterns of Price Movement

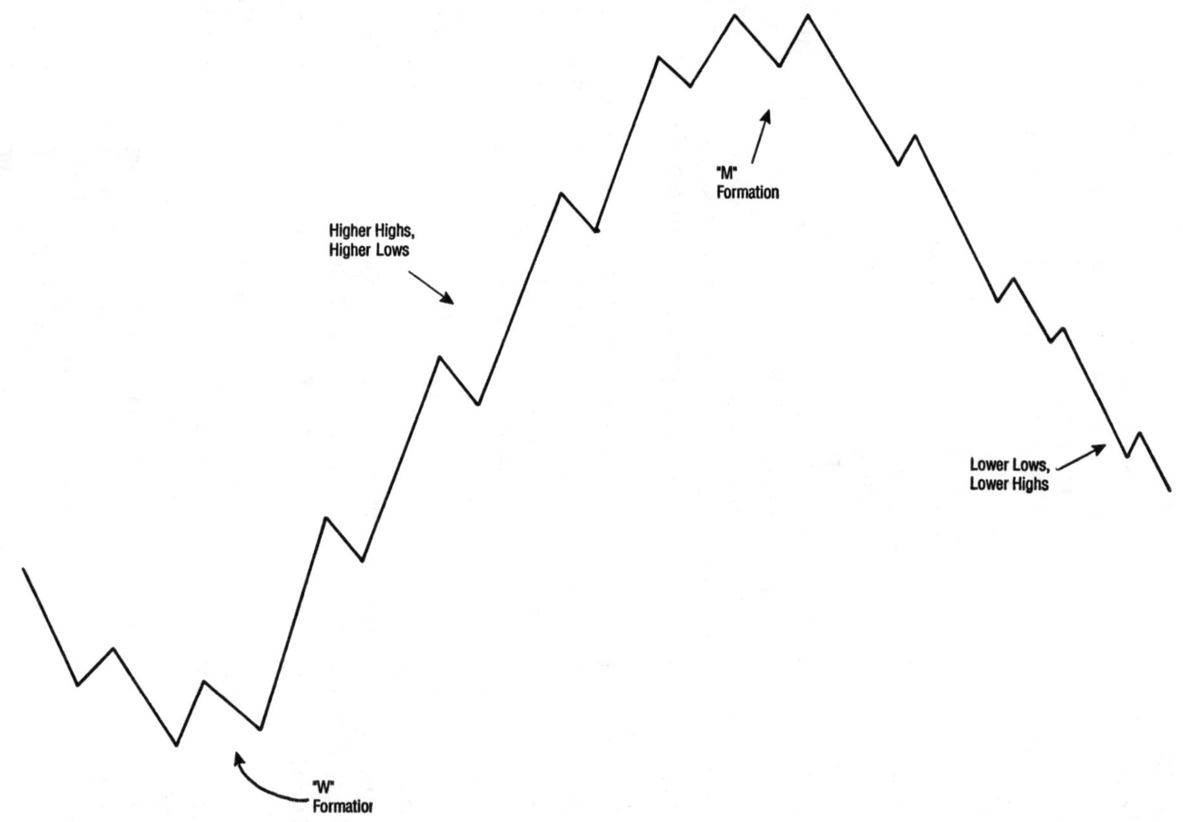

Lower Lows,
Lower Highs

"M"
Formation

Higher Highs,
Higher Lows

"W"
Formation

Figure 9-5 Use of Trend Lines to Determine Rising and Falling Prices

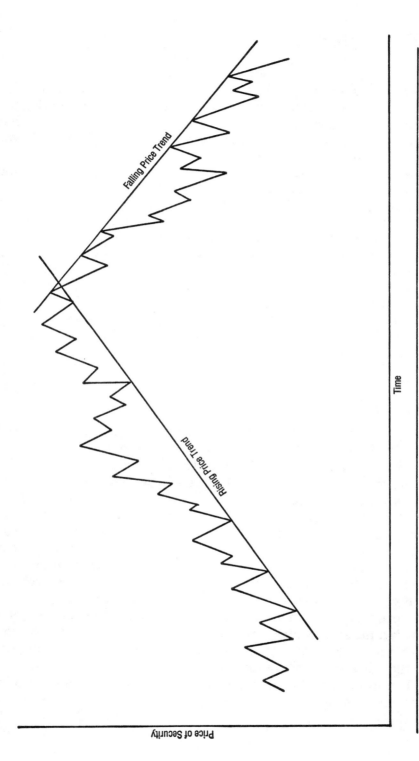

long as the actual price of the fund is above the moving average (this means the current price is higher than its average price for the last 40 weeks), an uptrend is defined. When it is below its moving average (its price is less that its average price for the last 40 weeks), a downtrend is defined.

A major advantage of the moving average technique is that its trend change signals are unambiguous. Judgment is not involved in the interpretation. When a crossing takes place the trend is defined from up to down. The major problem with this approach is in determining the sensitivity of trend definition. Long term moving averages define the major trend in prices, but are late in defining changes in trend. Short term moving averages quickly indicate changes in trend but suffer from the problem of whipsaws—rapid and "false" trend change indications. For the typical long-term investor, a moving average in the 30 to 50 week range usually provides a reasonable compromise between too many whipsaws and too late signals.

Excesses

Another technical approach for making predictions is the use of excess indicators. Prices of a security are sometimes driven up rapidly by over-enthusiasm and down quickly by excessive despair. When these extreme movements take place, a reversal in direction often takes place as sanity returns to the marketplace. One method for determining these excesses is to measure the difference between two moving averages. The result is what market technicians call "momentum"—a measure of the rate of change of price movement. When momentum increases significantly, a return to more normal levels can be expected as the underlying security changes trend.

Figure 9-7 displays momentum as an oscillator for the Financial Programs European mutual fund. The oscillator represents a 12 week difference between two 12 week moving averages. When momentum reaches an extreme level as defined by the crossing of one of the horizontal lines, a reversal in direction can be expected.

The upper and lower horizontal boundary lines and the moving average length are found empirically, based on past price behavior.

Figure 9-6   40 Week Moving Average for Trend Determination

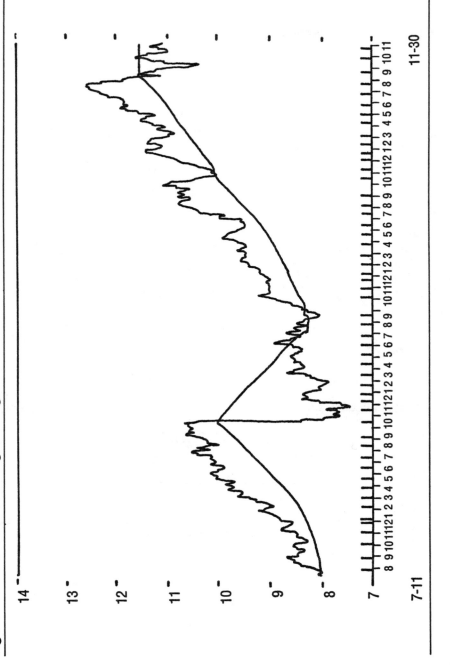

Figure 9-7   Excesses and The Momentum Oscillator

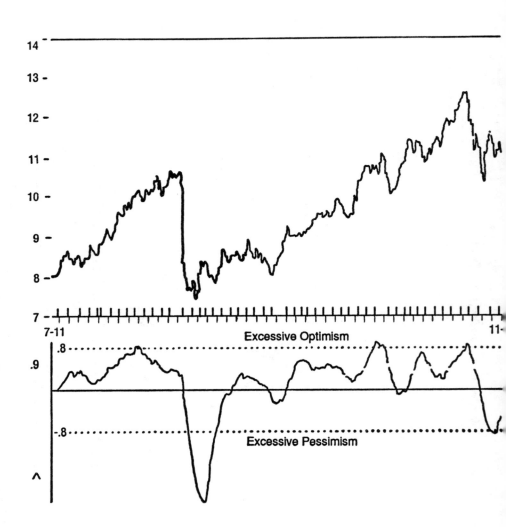

A different investment may require different parameters. A great advantage of using computer software is that many alternatives can be back-tested in just a few minutes.

The Relative Strength Index (RSI) is another popularly used indicator of excess price movements. Originated by J. Welles Wilder Jr. and found on most technical analysis software packages, it measures price excess on a common scale (0 to 100) for any financial instrument tracked. Figure 9-8 shows an example of this timing indicator used on the same mutual fund shown in the previous example.

When the index exceeds the 70 percent level, an excessive "overbought" condition is said to exist. When it falls below the 30 percent level, an excessive "oversold" condition is said to exist. In either case, a reversal becomes more probable when the levels are breached.

Divergences

The final evidence that comes from technical analysis that we will discuss is divergence. The objective of this approach is to discover financial variables that are expected to move in certain ways, but occasionally depart from "normal" behavior. The failure of these variables to maintain their normal relationships is used as an early warning indicator, indicating that a reversal in price movement is coming. Figure 9-9 provides a graph of Barron's World Index published weekly in the *International Trader* section of the magazine. Below the World Index (top chart) are charts of two technical measures previously discussed: momentum and RSI. As the chart shows, the momentum and RSI both fail to follow the index to new highs at the peak (point "A"), signaling caution and a general skepticism of the ability of prices to hold at the high.

A major advantage of using momentum and RSI for testing for divergences is that they can be used for any financial instrument that can be graphed, including equity indexes, individual stocks and bonds, bond averages, metals, interest rates, and mutual funds. It is simply a matter of plotting the indicators and assessing their movement vis-a-vis the security of interest.

Closed-end country funds possess a special type of divergence that can be useful as technical evidence to aid in the timing of their

Figure 9-8   Excesses and The Relative Strength Index (RSI)

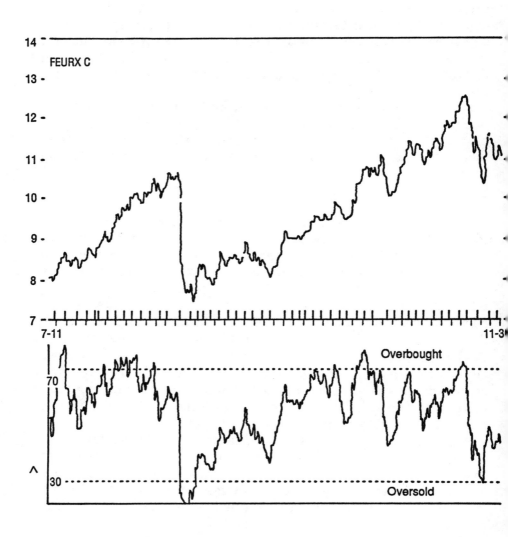

Figure 9-9   Divergences

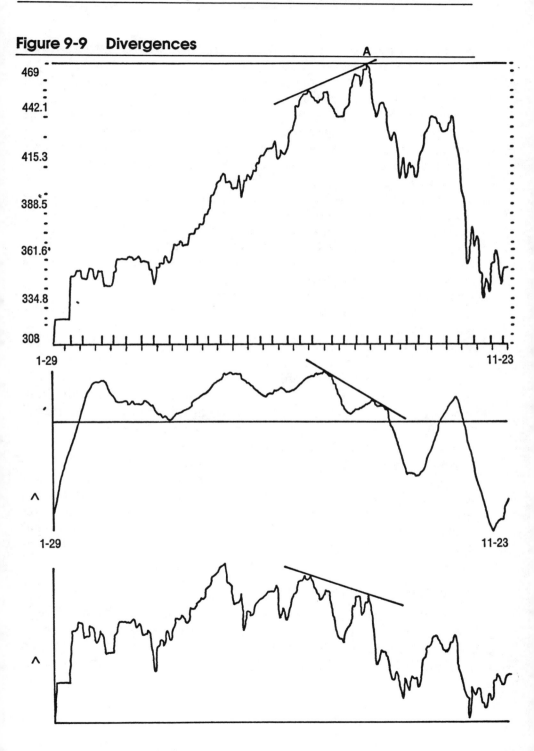

purchase and sale. As you remember from chapter two, these funds trade in the marketplace and fluctuate in price according to supply and demand. At any given point in time they can sell at a discount or premium to their net asset value. When there is a large negative divergence between the price of a fund and its asset value (a large discount), the divergence may be signaling an excessively pessimistic view of the future. When the discount shrinks or there is a comparatively large premium, an overly optimistic view exists.

As an example, assume a country fund has a net asset value of $15. Further assume that economic prospects for the country become bleak and the stock market falls, with the net asset value of the stocks held by the country fund dropping to $10. Being freely traded, the fund may fall to $8 owing to pessimism about the future. This price represents a 20 percent discount from its actual asset value. When the stock market rallies, the premium will likely shrink as optimism returns.

Seth Copeland Anderson, a Professor at the University of Alabama, studied the behavior of price divergences from net asset value in 17 closed-end mutual funds over a 20 year period. He found that there were a number of strategies that could be used to earn a profit on the divergences. The most consistent was to buy funds when selling at a 20 percent discount and later sell them when the discount narrowed to 15 percent. This approach produced a return of nearly 3,000 percent over the term of the study.

Barron's provides price and discount/premium data on all traded closed-end funds. Specialized country funds are found in the "Equity & Convertible Funds" section, International and global funds are found in the "Diversified Funds" section and global bond funds are found in the "Closed-End Bond Funds" section. The premium/discount information can be used as a solitary model to generate buy and sell signals, or it can be viewed as just another piece of evidence in the totality of the technical picture.

Other Technical Evidence

Besides the technical indicators discussed in this book, there is a considerable amount of additional technical evidence that can be used for timing purposes. Both *Barron's* Market Laboratory section and the *Investor's Daily* Psychological Indicator table provide additional possibilities for use in developing your own timing system. Furthermore, *The Encyclopedia of Technical Market Indicators* by Robert W. Colby and Thomas A. Meyers (Dow Jones-Irwin, 1988) and *The Wall Street Waltz* by Kenneth L. Fisher (Contemporary Books, 1987) are excellent resources for more information. *The Encyclopedia of Technical Market Indicators* gives an overview of over 110 indicators, along with their historical performance. *The Wall Street Waltz* provides 90 historical graphs showing relationships between indicators and stock market movements. Many of the indicators shown in the books can be easily adapted for use in a specific foreign market of interest.

COMPOSITE MODELS

A more sophisticated way to make use of technical indicators and business cycle information is to analytically combine the diverse data from each to make a composite mathematical model. The basic idea of creating a model is to put together the financial evidence in an unambiguous way so as to provide "signals" that identify favorable and unfavorable periods for investing. A major advantage of this approach is that subjectivity is removed from the operating decisions. Instead of weighing the evidence yourself to arrive at a decision, the model provides the decision point automatically.

Martin Zweig, in his book *Winning on Wall Street* (Warner, 1987) describes a simple two factor model which can be used for timing the purchase and sale of stocks. Although the model as described was intended for U.S. stocks, it can be adapted for use on stocks of any country. Essentially, the Zweig model attempts to combine a major economic cycle factor with a technical trend indicator. Stocks are held only when two conditions are met: 1) interest rates are declining as measured by a declining prime rate, and 2) stock prices are rising as measured by a four percent or more up-move from a weekly price index bottom. Figure 9-10 provides a pictorial view of how this model provides signals.

On U.S. stocks this model claimed a 12.6 percent annual return compared with the S&P 500 average annual performance of 9.1 per-

Figure 9-10 The Zweig Time Factor Model

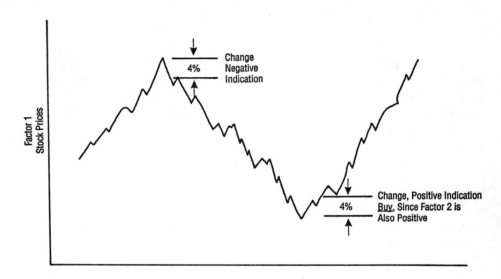

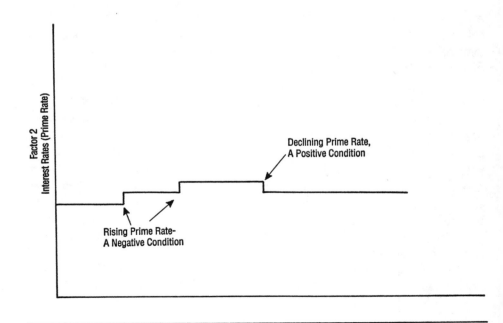

cent. As we saw in chapter two, even a small percentage increase in return over a long period of time can have a dramatic effect on an ending balance (Table 2-1), so this extra 3.5 percentage points are significant.

To use this approach on foreign stocks, it is necessary to track an interest rate within the country that is comparable to the U.S. prime lending rate, and monitor the movement of a broad market average. As an example, the Japanese market could be timed by using the Japanese prime rate and the 225 share Nikkei Index. Buy and sell signals would be generated in the same manner as shown in Figure 9-10. Since market average and interest rate data are available in Barron's, you will have no difficulty constructing the Japanese model or similar models for other major industrial countries. For more information and a historical record of this model we refer you to Zweig's book.

A more complex integrative stock timing model can be found in Dick A. Stoken's fascinating book, *Strategic Investment Timing.* Like the Zweig model, it was developed for the U.S. market but can be adapted to foreign markets. Stoken's model has four components: 1) interest rates (long and short term); 2) the Dow Jones Industrial Average; 3) the annual inflation rate; and 4) the current date in relation to the next presidential election. By combining these four pieces of evidence, Stoken's model has identified the beginning of each bull and bear market within an average of four percent of the exact high or low since 1921! The return from the model over this time period was 18.4 percent per year.

The Stoken model identifies a "buy" point when: 1) the investment climate is favorable *and* the stock market is in a buy zone; or 2) five months after the stock market has reached a five year low. A favorable investment climate occurs when either short-term (90 day T Bills) or long-term (AAA Corporate Bonds) interest rates fall to a 15 month low, *or* on October 1st, two years before the next presidential election. The stock market is said to be in a buy zone one week after the Dow Industrials closes at a two year low.

A "sell" point occurs when: 1) the investment climate turns hostile *and* the stock market is in a caution zone; or 2) seven months after the investment climate turns hostile; or 3) inflation climbs to a five percent annual rate and is the highest rate in a year. A hostile investment climate is one in which both short and long term interest rates are at seven year highs. A caution zone for the stock market occurs when the Dow closes at a two year high.

Stoken provides a rationale for the rules of his model, and discusses certain qualifications (for example, deflationary periods) in his book. If you would like to use his model on international markets, or have an interest in building your own unique integrative model, *Strategic Investment Timing* is must reading.

BOND MARKET MODELS

Timing models for an international bond fund or for bonds of a specific country typically make use of at least three factors; a trend indicator for interest rates, an inflation rate indicator, and a currency exchange rate indicator.

As we learned from the discussion of the business cycle, as interest rates decline, bond prices increase, and as interest rates rise, bond prices decline. Owing to this relationship, bonds are preferred for purchase when interest rates are in a downtrend. Inflation's effect on bonds is based on its linkage with interest rates. As inflation rises lenders demand higher interest to compensate them for the future loss in purchasing power. Higher interest rates in turn devalue the prices of existing bonds. Finally, as a country's currency value falls the cost of imported goods rise, contributing to inflation and higher interest rates.

A bond model that makes use of these factors is the *No-Load Portfolios* Newsletter Bond Climate Model (No-Load Portfolios, 8635 W. Sahara, Suite 420, The Lakes, NV 89117). For this model a point system is used to rate the status of each of the factors. The Dow Jones 20 Bond index is used as the indicator of interest rate movements. When it is above its 40 week moving average (interest rates are declining), three points are given to the model. The Producer Price Index (PPI) is used as the indicator of inflation rate trend. When it is below its 12 month moving average (inflation is declining), two points are provided to the bond model. The U.S. trade weighted dollar index is used as the currency value measure. When it is above its 40 week moving average (dollar is strengthening), two points are given to the model. Zero points are given for each of these factors when they are not in their favorable conditions. A buy signal occurs when the number of points from the three factors total five or more. This signal remains in effect until the total number of points drops to four points or less.

While the bond model just described is based on U.S. market data, it can be easily adapted to any country. It is only a matter of using interest rates, exchange rates, and inflation data applicable to the country of interest.

GOLD MARKET TIMING MODELS

Martin J. Pring, editor of the *Pring Market Review* (P.O. Box 338, Washington Depot, CT 06794) utilizes a four-factor gold timing model to determine favorable and unfavorable periods for holding gold. The model uses price trends in: 1) gold shares; 2) commodities; 3) currency; and 4) gold bullion. Rising commodity prices provide an inflationary backdrop for gold, and a falling dollar raises the prices of imported goods, further fueling inflation. Both are therefore important components of the model. Gold shares often rise before the price of gold itself as investors anticipate future financial events, so it has forecasting power. Finally, the trend in the price of gold bullion tends to persist over time, so it is used to predict further movements.

Like the bond market model previously discussed, the gold model uses a point system to determine when to buy and sell. When the Toronto Stock Exchange Gold Share Index is above its 12 week moving average, two points are given to the model. When the Economist All-Commodity Index is above its 12 month moving average, three points are provided. A downtrend in the Trade Weighted U.S. dollar index provides two points to the model and the price of London gold bullion adds seven points. When each of these four factors is trending in opposite directions, zero points are assigned. A buy signal arises when the model points sum to eight or more. The buy signal stays in effect until the sum of model points falls below eight points. The current status of this model is provided each month in the *Pring Market Review*.

Building Your Own Models

Many investors receive enjoyment from building their own unique timing models. If you choose to do so, the previously mentioned approaches provide a good starting point for proceeding. The first step is to choose the factors that you believe to be important for the market you wish to develop buy and sell signals for. It will be necessary to choose specific indicators whose value you have timely access to. In the international arena, this may force you to make compromises as the information you want may not be readily available. Whatever indicators you choose as model components, it is important to create unambiguous rules so you know precisely when to take action. After making your model it is important to back-test it to see how it worked in the past. It should not be too sensitive, so as to prevent an excessive amount of switches. Your model should be kept relatively simple (no more than six components) so it can be easily maintained. It is important to understand that whatever model you make, it certainly will not provide perfect results. Our world is a probabilistic one, and all we hope to achieve with our timing models is to put the odds of success in our favor.

REFERENCES

Seth, Anderson, "Closed-End Funds Versus Market Efficiency," *Journal of Portfolio Management*, Fall, 1986, p.63-65.

Band, Richard E., *Contrary Investing for the '90's* (New York, NY: St. Martin's Press, 1990).

Colby, Robert W., and Meyers, Thomas A. *The Encyclopedia of Technical Market Indicators* (Homewood, IL: Dow Jones-Irwin, 1988).

Gayed, Michael. *Intermarket Analysis and Investing* (New York, NY: Simon & Schuster, 1990).

Fisher, Kenneth L. *The Wall Street Waltz* (Chicago, IL: Contemporary Books, 1987).

Merriman, Paul A. and Dowd, Merle E., *Market Timing with No-Load Mutual Funds* (New York, NY: Henry Holt and Company, 1987).

Pring, Martin "Rebound in Gold," *Barron's*, March 3, 1986, p. 26-28.

Stoken, Dick A., *Strategic Investment Timing* (Chicago, IL: Probus Publishing, 1990).

The Individual Investor's Microcomputer Resource Guide (Chicago, IL: The American Association of Individual Investors, 1990).

Zweig, Martin, *Martin Zweig's Winning with New IRA's* (New York, NY: Warner Books, 1987).

CHAPTER 10

Buying Real Estate Abroad

It sounds like a dream. Buying a house or apartment for a song in a desirable foreign location like Paris, London or on the beach in the Costa del Sol, then living in the property for a month or two each year and renting it out (at a large profit) for the rest of each year. Eventually the property is sold, resulting in a sizable capital gain. Alternatively, purchasing office space in a booming foreign economy and renting it out to a local business enterprise, later selling it at a hefty profit. Are these realistic investment scenarios for the world-view investor? Perhaps, but there are many obstacles preventing real estate investment options from being anything but pipe dreams. In this chapter we hope to provide you with advice that will enable you to make informed decisions in the international real estate market.

FINDING THE RIGHT REAL ESTATE INVESTMENT

The first step in the foreign real estate purchase process is to ask yourself why you want to buy foreign property in the first place. There is certainly no shortage of opportunities for investment right here in the U.S., so why bother to look elsewhere? One reason is diversification. While the real estate market may stagnate or decline in one part of the world, it may increase steadily in another. Through multi-country investing it is possible to spread the overall risk of real estate investments through portfolio diversification.

217

Also, some regions of the world are going through, or will soon go through a phase of rapid economic growth. This offers the potential for dramatic real estate appreciation, much greater than could be expected in the U.S. A look back at Taiwan and Japan in the 1980's provides just two examples of soaring real estate markets. Finally, ownership of foreign real estate provides the opportunity (or excuse) to travel to your property to inspect, vacation, or even live there for an extended period of time. Obviously, your major objective in purchasing foreign real estate will have a bearing on where you will buy. If you are looking for a place to live, you will want to look at those areas that support your income and life style. If a pure business investment is what you have in mind, growth opportunities and levels of economic risk will predominate.

Finding specific foreign real estate opportunities can be difficult without personally visiting the country or countries of interest. There are, however, some steps that can be taken right here at home before venturing out of the country. The monthly newsletter *International Living*, (Agora, Inc. 824 E. Baltimore St., Baltimore, MD 21202) offers a rich source of information about living conditions and investments in foreign countries. Many of the accounts in this newsletter are written by Americans living in the countries they write about. Specific examples of foreign real estate purchases are provided each month, with actual prices and comments about the advantages and disadvantages of ownership. Although the major focus is on real estate investments for personal living purposes, commercial real estate investments are occasionally discussed. The newsletter also has a classified advertisement section with listed property for sale and a letters-to-the-editor section that often provides valuable information from readers concerning their foreign real estate experiences. The following list of recent article titles provides an idea of what this newsletter offers.

- "How to Own a Piece of the Costa de Sol"
- "My Mallorcan Paradise"
- "A Firsthand Guide to Property in the Algarve"
- "Ten Years of World-Wide Bargains in Real Estate"
- "Consider the Elegance of a French Chateau"
- "Invest in Baltic Real Estate?"

- "Interested in a Home in France? Look to Languedoc"
- "A Country Home in Ireland—a Bargain *and* a Good Investment"
- "Restore Mallorcan Farmhouses for Fun and Profit"
- "Greece— the Real Estate Buy of the 1990's"

This publication also provides an annual "Quality of Life Index," published in its January newsletter. All major countries of the world are given a summary score based on; 1) cost of living; 2) state of the economy; 3) political and civil rights; 4) political stability; 5) health; 6) infrastructure; and 7) culture and entertainment. The countries are ranked so you can see how your favorites measure up to the competition.

Another valuable source of information is the monthly magazine, *The International Property Times* (Fleece Yard Studios, Market Hill, Buckingham, England MK1815X). This monthly magazine is devoted to the purchase and sale of international real estate, with an emphasis on Europe. The magazine carries many full color photographs of properties for sale, both resale and new developments. It also provides an excellent source of addresses of foreign real estate agents. Along with property listings, each issue contains useful feature articles, like, "A Guide to Golf Development Properties World-Wide," and "Now is the Time to Realize Your Dream of Owning a Hotel or Restaurant in the French Countryside." The magazine is planning to publish special editions on three continents, including a separate German language issue.

Of lesser value than the previous references, but still worth looking at, are newspapers with international real estate listings. One such paper is the *International Herald Tribune*. Published in Paris and written in the English language, this paper is available throughout Europe and in the U.S. at many big-city newsstands and most major libraries. Reading the classified section of this newspaper over time can provide a good feeling for prices and availability of property throughout Europe.

The *New York Times* and *Los Angeles Times* are other newspapers with international property sections. The *Los Angeles Times* "Other Countries Property" section typically provides some property listings in Mexico and Canada. The "Vacation Leisure Homes" classified section of the *New York Times* often has listings for Europe and the Caribbean. For either paper, it is the Sunday edition that contains the most listings. It should be remembered that most of the listings in English language newspapers and most other English sources are being sold by English language sellers, primarily American. Better deals can often be found by expanding the search to encompass local sellers.

If you know what country you would like to invest in, or have narrowed the list of countries to just a few, local newspapers can be extremely valuable. Of course, local newspapers are published in the language of the country, so it may place an additional burden on you to translate the advertisements. Even if you can read the language, there may be specialized real estate terms or abbreviations that will require an extra effort from you to understand the meaning. Along with providing an idea of prices and availability of real estate, local papers often furnish you with the names and addresses of foreign real estate agents in the location of interest. If you are serious about making a real estate purchase, letters to three or four foreign real estate agents, outlining the type of property you are interested in, can bring a wealth of information and initial personal contacts that will be of value when you travel to the area.

The best way to find good investment property is the same way that one finds a good spouse: through a substantial period of personal "looking" aided by the recommendations of trusted others. Fortunate is the individual who has relatives or good friends in a foreign country where an investment is desired. They can perform much of the leg-work for you and can provide you with the kind of intimate knowledge that would be difficult (if not impossible) for you to obtain quickly on your own. The world over, foreigners are viewed with some suspicion; having a local connection can remove or reduce this barrier and pave the way for you to receive better overall treatment by the seller and the seller's agents. Whether or not you have this special connection, you should plan to make a considerable "hands-on" effort in the country of choice before committing yourself to a real estate purchase.

Many Americans have blood ties to other countries through parents, grandparents or great-grandparents. Special feelings may exist for a "distant homeland" through our knowledge of the language, customs, or known family relations. These ties give a special significance to foreign investing, and may provide both the comfort level and motivation to easily choose a specific country for making investments.

Residential Real Estate

The purchase of foreign residential real estate can provide you with the option of living in your investment as well as possible financial profit potential. Americans approaching retirement age may find that their retirement spent in a foreign country can provide them with a lifestyle that could not be matched in the United States. Many retirees find that the equity in their current house, coupled with savings, social security and pension income will allow them to purchase foreign property and still have enough money for maid service, travel, frequent dining out and other pleasures that would be difficult to maintain in the States. Moreover, life in a foreign country offers a measure of adventure that could not be matched at home. Examples (but not an exhaustive list) of some popular foreign locations that have attracted Americans in recent years are shown in Table 10-1. All of these countries have expatriot communities that can be very helpful for the would-be buyer of residential property. Some American enclaves have clubs and newsletters that can be a useful information source even if you wish to buy property outside of the "American zone."

Buying property primarily for lifestyle enhancement is a strategy that does not depend on price appreciation as the ultimate measure of investment success. Since you are living in the property, even if it does not meet your appreciation expectations, you are still receiving benefit from it. It is, however, a strategy that is not without significant risk to the buyer.

Life in a foreign country can turn out to be different than expected. As we mentioned previously, in many countries the foreigner is viewed with much suspicion. While it is easy in America to move into a neighborhood and quickly make friends, in many foreign countries it may be much more difficult to find acceptance from the locals. While we Americans move from place to place throughout our lives, many foreigners tend to stay put. Generations may live in the same neighborhood, and anyone who is not a fam-

Table 10-1 Some Popular Foreign Locations
for Residential Real Estate Purchases

Country	Area
Andorra	Andorra la Vella
Australia	New South Wales (near Sidney) Nambucca Heads, Perth, Tasmania (Hobart)
Bahamas	Freeport, Nassau
Canada	Vancouver area, Toronto area, Nova Scotia
Caribbean	Bahamas, U.S. Virgin Islands, Puerto Rico, St. Lucia,
China	Fujian
Costa Rica	San Jose
France	Paris area, Cote d'Azur
Great Britain	London, Southwest Peninsula North Wales, Scotland
Greece	Athens area (Glyfada)
Israel	Haifa, Harzilya
Italy	Italian Riviera, Lake District Tuscany
Mexico	Baja, Guadalajara
Portugal	Algarve
Spain	Costa del Sol, El Escorial Madrid (Northern suburbs)
Taiwan	Tien-moo area

ily member is viewed as an outsider. Socialization is often impeded by perceptions of differences in family status and language problems. Being good neighbors in many countries means avoiding or ignoring "outsiders." Moreover, you may find foreign living to be a difficult challenge. Possibly inadequate medical care and schooling, and the loss of easy visitation with stateside relatives and friends can be too much for some expatriots to bear. An initial idyllic setting in the countryside can easily turn to boredom after a few months. Since many foreign countries have severe restrictions on working, you may find it to be difficult to find satisfaction from work that you may be accustomed to. The home itself is another problem. Many homes in foreign countries have no central heating or cooling. The construction may be of very poor quality when viewed from an American perspective. Damp, dark, and breezy are the words often used to describe the interiors of many foreign dwellings, especially those near the shoreline. If you buy an apartment you may find the walls seem to be nearly paper thin. This is especially troublesome if the neighbor's children only have time to practice their musical instruments after 11 p.m., or if the family fights constantly. If you buy in a vacation area, as many Americans do, you may find that during the vacation season the town is filled with tourists, but when the tourist season is over, restaurants and shops are boarded up and closed until the start of the next tourist season. There are either too many people, preventing you from enjoying the area, or too few people, leading to a virtual shut-down of the entire area. Table 10-2 provides a summary of these (and other) possible problems that you might encounter. Of course one of the best ways to avoid possible negative surprises is to move to the area and live in rental housing for a number of months before making a commitment.

Instead of buying residential property and living in it full time, it is also possible to buy and rent it out. It could be rented out throughout the year, or, alternatively, you could live in the property a few weeks (or months) out of the year and rent it out the rest of the time. This strategy is only possible, of course, if your property is located in a desirable area for rental occupancy. Beach-front property, downtown property in a desirable big-city destination, and mountain resort property are all examples of possibilities. The

Table 10-2 Potential Obstacles in Successful Foreign Real Estate Ownership

Difficult to locally finance
Difficult to sell in the domestic marketplace
Illiquid
Political risk
Currency exchange risk
Difficult absentee control
Rent control laws (can't get tenants out or restrictions
    on increases in rent)
Property, transfer and other taxes
Zoning restrictions on where property can be purchased
Bureaucracy in getting permits for making improvements
Lower standards of design and construction
Large capital gains tax on sale of property
Large closing costs
Protracted time to close
Required under-the-table payments and payoffs
Laws restricting the personal use of your residence
Difficulty in finding a reliable, unbiased broker
Language problems

major problem you will have in implementing this strategy is obtaining reliable control over the renters while you are away. Nothing is better than a personal reference from a trusted other who has knowledge of an honest and effective real estate manager. Some foreign real estate brokers specialize in selling and managing properties for non-residents. If you can obtain the names and addresses of a few of the property owners they deal with, and contact the owners directly, you will be able to get an impression of the agent as well as the feasibility of buying and renting out from afar.

Another problem with renting residential property is with rent control. Many countries have very strong rent control laws making it virtually impossible to evict anyone from rental property as long as an attempt is made by the tenant to pay the rent. Furthermore, the maximum amount of rent increase may be established by law. Over time this may result in cash flow losses for the property, which may only be remedied by selling or walking away from the property.

One option that many Americans have made use of is the purchase of foreign real estate through time-share units. This mode of purchase allows an investor to buy time in a unit, usually for a specific week or number of weeks each year. As an example a typical weekly time-share unit might cost $10,000 to purchase and, in addition, annual fees for maid service, taxes and upkeep of about $220. In a majority of time-share ownership agreements, the time-share unit can potentially be sold or traded with other time-share owners in different locations. Mexico has been a favorite place for American foreign time-share ownership. As tourists, they have been the target of sales pitches extolling the time-share concept of cheap lifetime vacations. Unfortunately, many property owners have become disillusioned with this approach to real estate ownership. After a few years, a timeshare owner may become tired of visiting Puerto Vallerta on week 23. Moreover, the annual maintenance fees of these resorts tend to go up over time. A $199 annual fee at the time of purchase may seem reasonable, but five years later the annual fee may have risen to an "unreasonable" $400.

In general, timeshare units do not make economic sense as an investment, and often they do not make sense even as a way to vacation cheaply. For those who like the timeshare concept but want to improve the economic picture significantly, purchasing timeshare units through the resale market may be the way to go. Many previous timeshare buyers want to get out from under their purchase at most any reasonable price. Purchases can sometimes be made at one-fourth to one-half the original sales price. A number of timeshare resale brokers are available which can provide you with current listings. Timeshare Resale International (Harrisonberg VA, 800-368-3541), Timeshare Travel (Salt Lake City, UT, 800-367-3799), and Condolink (Omaha, NE, 800-877-9600), are some examples. One strategy for buyers with flexible schedules is to buy an "undesirable" timeshare (for example, a hot summer week in a desert community) in the resale market at a very cheap price, then arrange for last-minute trades in better locations. Of course, this approach can only be done with those timeshare exchange services that have a last-minute pool of exchanges that are available for *any* offering in return.

Commercial Real Estate Investment

Along with residential real estate, commercial property offers another possible foreign investment opportunity. Investing in commercial property is often a riskier investment requiring greater capital and its success is tied more directly to the ups and downs of the local economy than residential real estate. This added risk makes it essential that a very thorough personal effort be made in securing the right property.

One strategy for making a foreign commercial real estate investment is to locate an area that is currently undergoing a rapid economic expansion, then buy commercial property in a business area and lease it out to a local business organization. As an absentee owner, your objective would be to sell the property at a profit after a few years of rapid price appreciation. This strategy works best during the early phase of an economic expansion in cities with a commercial real estate market that is not overburdened with vacancies. Successful implementation therefore requires a knowledge of both local business conditions and local commercial real estate conditions.

A second approach to selecting a country for investing is based on a contrary positioning strategy. This is the same type of strategy for real estate that some stock market investors use to choose common stocks. The basic idea is to buy when prospects appear bleak and no one is buying (prices are low), and sell when the majority of investors are buying (prices are high). To implement this approach successfully takes a good feel for timing. If you buy too soon prices may continue to drop or languish at a low level, and you may have to wait years to see a profit.

There is of course a whole spectrum of problems that affect real estate prices. There are those countries or areas of the world that seem to have chronic economic problems, the real "basket cases" of the world. Others have serious but seemingly more temporary problems.

Examples of chronic and severe problems are a multi-decade civil war, or an entrenched dictator whose primary concern is self aggrandizement at the expense of the entire economy. Examples of temporary problems are a deep recession that appears to be cyclic in nature or economic problems brought on by a singular event, such as a shortage of oil or an "act of God" such as a hurricane or earthquake.

Where are some areas of the world that currently fit the image of chronic problems? Examples include Lebanon with its terrible civil war, and Northern Ireland with the IRA. Another example is the Philippines with communist rebels and political instability. Other examples abound that are chronic but less severe in their magnitude than those just mentioned. When Cuba adopts meaningful democratic and market changes, this close-by potential vacation and business destination can be expected to show dramatic growth. As political changes in the 1990's continue take place in other centrally planned economies such as Russia, China and South-East Asia, we can expect many more opportunities to develop. South America also provides possibilities. Brazil and Argentina, with their massive foreign debt load and poor domestic economic conditions make them currently very unattractive for making a commercial real estate purchases. It is possible, however, that the economies of these countries could turn around if their inflation rates are brought under control and debt relief occurs. More immediate in their prospects for investment are the Eastern European countries that have recently shed the burden of communism. When substantial economic growth commences, the commercial real estate market can be expected to advance smartly.

In any case, the basic idea is to identify economically troubled countries and "basket cases" of the world and have the patience to wait for better times. All the time you are waiting you are learning all you can about the country, its real estate and the possibility for a comeback. If you have family ties to one of these countries you are in an excellent position to get first-hand, reliable information on how the events are unfolding. In many of these countries, better times come in an uneven manner, with some parts of the country improving while others continue to languish. It is important to be able to accurately assess the overall situation, and know when and where to make your move. In general, you will want to buy the very best property that you can possibly afford, as this has the best chance of rebounding in price when things get better. If you make a mistake and buy too soon, you may at least end up with the feeling that your great-grandchildren will be thankful to you for having made the investment.

What problems can be expected for those attempting to buy foreign commercial real estate using either the "growth" or "contrarian" approach? Plenty. Just making the purchase may present an insurmountable challenge. In some countries certain areas of the country may be off-limits to foreign investors, and these are often the very best areas for investing. An overseas investment may also require a foreign partner, a move that adds more uncertainty to the investment. Moreover, some countries do not permit the outright sale of land to foreigners but may instead allow for only the purchase of a specific-term lease or "land-use rights." This can complicate the purchase and make a later resale more difficult.

Another potential problem lies with foreign real estate agents. You may find that they are not very helpful. Real estate agents work for the seller, not the buyer. As such, it may be impossible to get objective information about the property from this source. This is especially true if you are viewed as a foreigner having "deep pockets." Moreover, the oppressive bureaucracy in many countries, coupled with the necessity to provide substantial monetary "tips" to government officials to get anything done, is often enough to discourage would-be investors. Even after the investment is made, serious problems remain. As with rental residential real estate, the problem of control becomes critical. Who will manage the property for you while you are away? While there are management agencies available in most countries, you run the risk of having inflated repair bills and possible hold-backs of revenues received by the agency from the renter.

Even if these obstacles are surmounted, you will find additional risks due to currency fluctuations and political instability. If for example, the currency of the country falls dramatically with respect to the U.S. dollar, the value of your property would also drop, if you wished to sell and get your money out in U.S. dollars. Political factors can make for additional risk in a number of ways. If the government should pass a law making it more difficult for foreigners to buy property, then your sale would have to be confined to the local market, likely affecting the price negatively. Other local laws could also prove injurious. A strong rent control law which freezes rents for a period of years would make it extremely difficult to sell a property with a small positive cash flow, especially when combined with a history of rising property taxes. Exchange controls represent another potential problem. A country may adopt laws that may prevent you from repatriating profits from renting or selling your real estate and will obviously make the investment much less attractive.

FINANCING

In the United States it is a relatively easy proposition to apply for a real estate loan, and approval or denial can come fairly quickly. On a global basis this represents an exception rather than the typical course of affairs. For the vast majority of foreign real estate investments made by an individual investor, cash is the preferred method of financing. If a loan is needed, it may be better to get the loan in the U.S. based on equity in U.S. real estate or some other asset, rather than attempting to get the loan in the country where the investment is made.

Not only is it difficult to obtain real estate loans in most foreign countries, but loan payments will have to be made in the currency of the country where the loan was made. If the U.S. dollar depreciates against the foreign currency, you will find that your payments may increase substantially in dollars, even though the terms of the loan have not changed. Of course the opposite effect would occur if the dollar strengthened against currency of the load, i.e., loan payments would decrease.

BUILDING VERSUS BUYING

Those who have built their own home or a commercial building in the United States know the difficulties involved in such an endeavor. Subcontractors who do not show up on time, cost overruns, shoddy workmanship, the wrong or poor materials used, difficulty in getting inspectors to timely approve work done, the inability to get workers to come back out after work is completed but improperly done, and so on. Now imagine the situation in a foreign country where the subcontractors think you are infinitely wealthy, where you have difficulty communicating, where there are material shortages, where a full day's work is thought to be 4 hours, not eight, where gifts to inspectors may be expected.

In short, building in a foreign country may be a very difficult task, especially if you are on a tight budget and are in a hurry. The best way to approach this situation if you want to build is to find a general contractor who has a reputation for good and honest work and work with him. Preferably the contractor should have worked with other foreigners in the past so you can interview them.

SELLING YOUR PROPERTY

Compared with U.S. real estate, foreign real estate tends to be less liquid. This is especially true with residential real estate. As stated previously, we Americans are mobile, moving from place to place every few years. This tends not to be true with most foreigners, who tend to stay put. The market for residential real estate is therefore much thinner in foreign countries. Moreover, much real estate purchased by Americans tend to be in "foreign" areas, which means sales might have to be restricted to foreigners only, cutting down further on the size of the market.

Beyond the market for the property, laws in the country may restrict you from taking your money out of the country. There also may be large (by U.S. standards) capital gains taxes, which can take a substantial gain and shrink it to a puny one.

REAL ESTATE MUTUAL FUNDS

Instead of buying property directly, it is possible to buy into a mutual fund that has foreign real estate holdings. Table 10-3 provides a listing of such mutual funds.

Table 10-3 Mutual Funds with Foreign Property Holdings

Arbuthnot Finance and Property Share Fund
(U.K. Properties)
Arbuthnot Securities Ltd.
37 Queen St.
London EC4R 1BY England

Barclays Unicorn Financial Trust
(U.K. Properties)
Barclays Unicorn Group, Ltd.
Unicorn House, 252 Romford Road
London E7 9JB England

Britannia Properties Shares Trust
(U.K. Properties)
Britannia Group of Unit Trusts, Ltd.
Salisbury House, 31 Finsbury Circus
London EC2M 5QL England

Canada-Immobil
(Toronto Properties)
Societe Internationale de Placements
Elisabethenstrasse 41
4010 Basle, Switzerland

Interswiss
(Properties in Switzerland)
Societe Internationale de Placements
Elisabethenstrasse 41
4010 Basle, Switzerland

Rodamco IP
(Commercial Properties in the Netherlands)
Rotterdamsch Beleggingconsortium NV
Heer Bokelweg 25
3032 AD Rotterdam, The Netherlands

(Continues)

Table 10-3 (Continued)

Save and Prosper Scotbits
(International Properties)
Save and Prosper Group, Ltd.
4 Great St. Helens
London EC3P 3EP England

Schlesinger Property Shares Trust
(U.K. Properties)
Britannia Group of Unit Trusts, Ltd.
Salisbury House, 31 Finsbury Circus
London, EC2M 5QL England

Swissimmobil
(Properties in large cities in Switzerland)
Societe Internationale de Placements
Elisabethenstrasse 41
4010 Basle, Switzerland

Swissreal-A and Swissreal-B
(Swiss Real Estate)
Intrag AG
c/o Union Bank of Switzerland
PO Box 8021
Zurich, Switzerland

Tyndall/London Wall Financial Priority Units
(U.K. Properties)
Tyndall Managers Ltd.
18 Canynge Road
Bristol BS99 7UA England

It is essential to obtain a prospectus and study it very carefully before making a purchase decision. Many foreign property funds carry mortgages as well as actual real estate holdings, so fund value may not be tied directly to real estate appreciation. The type of real estate holdings also vary from fund to fund, with resort properties, office buildings and residential properties representing common alternatives. Moreover, the age of holdings differs greatly; some funds hold old real estate while others contain newer properties.

The potential buyer of a foreign fund should also be aware that regulations of fund management companies vary from country to country, and this may provide an additional risk in their purchase.

For some investors, the advantages of buying a real estate mutual fund outweigh buying the property directly. All the details regarding selection, purchase, rental and maintenance are handled by professionals within the country, so you do not have to get involved. Moreover, fund shares offer greater diversification and liquidity, which lowers the level of risk for small investors. For others, however, these same advantages may be viewed as limitations. Mutual funds are essentially sterile investments. For many, part of the enjoyment of property ownership comes from the hands-on involvement with the investment process. Moreover, unlike your own property, mutual fund properties cannot be lived in. Wide diversification in real estate often insures mediocre results, while a well positioned individual purchase may result in an immediate and substantial profit.

ALTERNATIVES TO REAL ESTATE OWNERSHIP

If your purpose in buying foreign real estate is to have a place to live, an alternative approach that will meet your goal (but not as an investment) is to rent instead of buy. This may be a sensible approach to take early on, even if you anticipate a real estate purchase will eventually be made.

Another alternative, if your objective is a vacation home, is to exchange your home with someone in the country where you wish to go. The exchange may be made based on personal contacts or through an exchange organization. Two reliable home exchange organizations are *Home Exchange International* (185 Park Row, P.O. Box 878, New York, NY 10038-0272 (212) 349-5340) and Intervac, P.O. 3975, San Francisco, CA 94119 (415) 435-3497).

REFERENCES

A Guide to Buying Property in Portugal, Russell and Russell, 9/13 Wood Street, Bolton B11EE, England, 1989.

Cooper, Marian, *The World's Top Retirement Havens* (Baltimore, MD: Agora Books, 1989).

International Living Newsletter, 824 E. Baltimore St., Baltimore, MD 21202.

International Property Times, Fleece Yard Studios, Market Hill, Buckingham, England MK181JX.

Island Properties Report, Gene Cowell, P.O. Box 88, Woodstock, VT 05019.

Scott, Gary A. and Robin Harris, *Worldwide Directory of Mutual Funds* (INEX Publishing, 1985).

The Whole World Catalog (Baltimore, MD: Agora, Inc., 1990).

CHAPTER 11

Tax Sheltered Accounts

We have discussed throughout this book that diversification through the use of international investments is one way to improve investment performance. Another strategy which can be combined with world wide investing is the use of tax sheltered accounts. We will discuss five types of tax sheltered programs: individual retirement accounts, simplified employee pension plans, Keogh plans, 401(k) plans and 403(b) plans.

Tax sheltered accounts offer two basic advantages. First, they allow the individual to defer the payment of income taxes until the money is taken out of the account at some time in the future, usually after retirement. Second, investors can often invest "before tax" dollars in such programs. These two characteristics mean that individuals can save money at the time of initial investment and throughout the time the money is invested. You should note, for example, that not all programs provide both advantages. Individual retirement accounts, for example, allow some people but not all to invest "before tax" dollars, depending on their level of income and whether they have a retirement plan at their place of employment.

The programs also have certain disadvantages. The most common criticism of them is that money is tied up for a long time. The funds usually are not available until 59 1/2 years of age except in cases of disability and certain other special circumstances.

Early withdrawal of the money results in tax liabilities and a 10 percent financial penalty. Also, the deferral of taxes always involves some risk. There is no way of knowing what tax rates will be in the future. Avoiding a 28 percent tax rate today in order to pay a 35 percent or 40 percent tax rate at some time in the future is hardly a good deal! Nevertheless, selecting worldwide investments as part of a diversified portfolio and then investing them in tax sheltered programs is a good step toward financial security.

INDIVIDUAL RETIREMENT ACCOUNTS

Individual retirement accounts give the individual the opportunity to put up to $2,000 a year into a tax deferred account where the funds can continue to grow on a tax deferred basis until retirement at age 59 1/2 or later. If husband and wife are both employed and earning at least $2,000 per year then each of them is eligible to have an IRA. If only one member of a married couple is employed they may put up to $2,250 a year into spousal IRA's.

If an IRA is an individual's *only* retirement plan, that individual can deduct the IRA contribution from income on the current year's tax return. Individuals who participate in an employer-maintained retirement plan may still deduct their contributions if their income does not exceed certain amounts, generally $25,000 for single taxpayers and about $40,000 for married couples filing jointly.

Money contributed to an IRA may be placed in almost any type of investment—savings accounts, certificates of deposit, stocks, bonds, mutual funds, real estate, etc. The main type of investment which cannot be placed in an IRA is collectibles—stamp collections, rare coins, art, etc. There was a time when gold could not be placed in an IRA, but the law has been changed so that one type of gold investment, the American Eagle gold coin, can now be used as an IRA investment.

Individuals may begin to withdraw funds from an IRA at the age of 59 1/2. They may withdraw all or some portion of the money in their IRA, and they pay tax on only that amount withdrawn in a given year. Dollars which were tax deductible when invested in the IRA will be subject to taxation when withdrawn. Dollars which were not tax deductible at the time of investment will not be subject to tax at the time of withdrawal. Taxpayers contributing to IRA's will file Form 8606 each year with their income tax forms. This will enable them to document which withdrawals are taxable and which are tax exempt.

The investor who chooses to withdraw funds early, i.e. before age 59 1/2, will be penalized. The funds withdrawn will be subject to the regular income tax level in the year they are withdrawn and in addition will be subject to a 10 percent penalty. There are exceptions which allow for withdrawals prior to age 59 1/2. These include permanent disability, certain medical expenses, equal withdrawals over the life of the individual and withdrawals by individuals separated from service after age 55. The requirements to qualify for these exceptions are subject to quite specific definition by the Internal Revenue Service. Individuals considering early withdrawal of IRA funds should consult a tax advisor.

Individuals must begin withdrawing funds from their IRA no later than the end of the year in which they reach age 70 1/2. They must withdraw a specific minimum amount each year based on the life expectancy tables used by the Internal Revenue Service. Failure to withdraw the required amount after age 70 1/2 will result in a tax penalty of 50 percent of the amount they should have withdrawn but did not.

Individuals have the right to contribute to an IRA from January 1 of any given year until April 15 of the following year. For example, a contribution for 1992 could be made as late as April 15, 1993. The timing of investments can be important, and earlier investments can make a major difference in results. Table 12-1 shows the difference in an annual $2,000 IRA investment made January 1 and the same investment made December 31 of that year. As noted, the difference is over $11,000 after 20 years of investing and the amount exceeds $88,500 after 40 years.

It is worth noting that one does not have to invest in an IRA every year nor is it necessary to invest $2,000. A person who can afford to invest only a few hundred dollars a year in an IRA has the right to do so. $2,000 is simply the maximum contribution allowed. There are mutual funds which have no required minimum deposit, and they are good vehicles for IRA contributions by the person who has only small amounts to invest.

Table 11-1   Results of IRA Investments Made at Different Times

End of Year	Investments Made On Jan. 1	Investments Made On Dec. 31	Difference
1	$ 2,200	$ 2,000	$ 200
5	13,431	12,210	1,221
10	35,062	31,875	3,187
15	69,900	63,545	6,355
20	126,005	114,550	11,455
25	216,364	196,694	19,670
30	361,887	328,988	37,899
35	596,254	542,049	54,205
40	973,704	885,186	88,518

Note: Assumes a 10% rate of return on Investments.

SIMPLIFIED EMPLOYEE PENSION PLAN

Simplified employee pension plans are sometimes called SEP-IRA's because they enable an employer to contribute money to an individual retirement account for an employee. As the name implies, it provides employers a relatively simple way to provide for employee retirement needs as well as for their own.

Funds may be contributed to a SEP-IRA in two ways. The employer can make contributions and the employee can elect to have a portion of salary contributed, in which case the taxes are deferred on the salary funds going into the account. The maximum amount going into the account may not exceed 15 percent of salary or $30,000, whichever is less. The maximum amount of that which can come from salary reduction is about $8,000 (the amount changes annually based on inflation).

The program is designed to insure that employers do not design the plans to favor themselves to the detriment of their employees. Employers creating such programs must cover all employees who are at least 21 years of age, make a certain minimum salary (which changes annually based on inflation) and have worked for the employer during three of the past five years. Contributions do not have to be made every year, but when they are made, they must be made to all eligible employees' accounts and the percentage contributed must be uniform for all employees.

The rules for withdrawal of funds from a SEP-IRA are similar to those for an IRA. One interesting exception is that individuals who are still actively employed after the age of 70 1/2 may continue to participate in their employer's SEP. Individuals may not contribute to their own individual IRA after that age.

KEOGH PLANS

Self-employed individuals have the option of establishing KEOGH plans rather than SEP's. If the individual has employees, the plan must be designed to cover them also. There are two types of KEOGH plans, defined contribution plans and defined benefit plans.

A defined-contribution plan is one in which contributions made to the plan must be consistent with certain legal requirements, and the amount one will ultimately receive after retirement depends on the investment results of the funds invested in the plan. A defined-benefit plan states the amount the worker will ultimately receive as income during retirement, and those amounts must be within certain established limits. Contributions to the plan are based on the amount needed to produce the stated benefits.

Defined-contribution plans are of two types, either profit-sharing plans or money-purchase plans. In profit-sharing plans, the contributions are based on a percentage of each participant's compensation. The percentage can be changed each year, and if there is a year in which there are no profits, then no contributions need to be made. A money-purchase plan also provides for contributions based on a percentage of compensation, but that percentage cannot be varied and contributions must be made each year whether or not there are profits.

The limit on contributions to both profit-sharing plans and money-purchase plans is the lower of 25 percent of compensation or $30,000. There is no specific limit on contributions to a defined benefit plan, but the amount of benefits that may be received in a given year is limited. The maximum annual benefit which may be received is the participant's average compensation for his or her three highest consecutive years of employment, up to a maximum of $90,000 (indexed for inflation).

Keogh plan distributions are subject to the same general limitations which apply to other retirement programs as discussed above. A Keogh plan must be established by the end of the year for which the contributions are made. Contributions may be made any time up to the due date for filing the employer's tax return.

401(k) PLANS

Section 401(k) plans, named for the section of the tax code where they are described, allow an employee to choose to have a portion of his or her income contributed directly to a retirement plan. The employer may or may not match a portion of the contributions. Contributions to these plans are tax deferred but they are subject to the FICA (Social Security) tax. The maximum amount an employee can choose to have tax-deferred annually is about $8,000 (indexed for inflation).

A unique advantage of 401(k) plans is that you can usually maintain control over how your funds are invested. Under most such plans, an employer will provide perhaps three or four options, which might include stock and bond mutual funds, an annuity option, etc. You, as the employee, can then choose how to allocate your retirement funds among these options. Moving your funds from one option to another does not involve any tax consequences so long as the funds are left within the plan. Some 401(k) plans allow participants to borrow from the funds, and there is no tax liability so long as the funds are repaid with interest within five years. You will need to check with your employer to see if your plan allows for loans.

When you leave your employer, if you do not immediately need your 401(k) funds for retirement purposes, you can roll over these funds into a regular IRA. Taxes continue to be deferred until you withdraw the funds for current use. Section 401(k) plans are generally subject to the same distribution restrictions as other retirement plans, including the imposition of a 10% penalty for early withdrawal prior to age 59 1/2 (except in cases of disability, etc.).

403(b) PLANS

Section 403(b) plans are similar to 401(k) plans, but they are designed specifically for employees of educational and other nonprofit organizations. They are also referred to as *tax sheltered annuity plans*. Under these plans, the employee agrees to have current salary reduced, or to forgo a salary increase, so that the employer can contribute that amount to a 403(b) plan. This enables the employee to put pre-tax dollars into the retirement plan.

The limitations on contributions are rather complicated, depending on whether the funds come entirely from salary reduction or are partly contributed by the employer. Salary reduction plans are limited in most cases to $9,500 a year. Contributions above that amount are considered to be taxable compensation. You should ask your employer to calculate the exact limit that applies to your specific case.

As with 401(k) plans, most 403(b) plans offer the participant several options. This allows the participant to choose among stock, bond and other investment alternatives. Distribution rules and limit- ations are essentially the same as for other retirement plans.

COORDINATING RETIREMENT FUNDS AND OTHER FUNDS

It is important to remember that money in your retirement plans is part of your overall portfolio. Investment strategies should keep that fact in mind. For example, the general theme of this book is the importance of global diversification in your investment decisions. You may find that the investment options offered to you in your retirement plan are all domestic investments. This may call for you to place even more emphasis on global investments in your other portfolio holdings.

Suppose you have decided you want to keep 20 percent of your portfolio in foreign investments. Assume also that you have $100,000 of investments, as follows:

Investments in retirement plans	$60,000
Other investments	40,000

If the options made available to you by your employer through a 401(k) or 403(b) plan are all investments in domestic securities, then you would have to achieve your 20 percent foreign allocation entire out of the funds over which you have control. That would mean investing $20,000, or 50 percent of the amount you control, overseas.

There are two other points to remember here. First, note that in your personal IRA you have complete control over what is invested there. You can select as many different foreign stocks, funds, etc. as you want for inclusion in your IRA. So long as these are U.S. traded securities or U.S. based mutual funds they may be placed in your IRA. Second, you can urge your employer to make an international fund one of the options available through your 401(k) or 403(b) plan. With an increasing portion of the investment opportunities being overseas, you can make a convincing argument to your employer that you should not be denied access to these opportunities when investing your retirement funds.

REFERENCES

Donoghue, William E., *Donoghue's Investment Tips for Retirement Savings* (New York, NY: Harper and Row, 1986).

Grace, William J., Jr., *The ABC's of IRA's* (New York, NY: Dell Publishing, 1982).

Lochray, Paul J., *The Financial Planner's Guide to Estate Planning* (Englewood Cliffs, NJ: Prentice-Hall, 1987).

Vicker, Ray, *The Dow Jones-Irwin Guide to Retirement Planning* (Homewood, IL: Dow Jones-Irwin, 1987).

Zweig, Martin, *Winning With New IRA's* (New York, NY: Warner Books, 1987).

APPENDIX A

Currency Exchange Factors

Buying a foreign security directly is not unlike buying a watch or other item in a foreign country. First you must convert the asking price into dollars in order to determine its cost to you in your money. Of course for an item like a watch it is also necessary to add in any taxes, duty and other costs to arrive at the total cost before making the purchase decision. With the direct purchase of a foreign security the process is essentially the same; total the relevant costs and make the conversion. Fortunately, exchange rates are readily available, so the conversion calculations can easily be made.

Currency exchange rates are presented daily in *The Wall Street Journal, Investor's Daily* and many big-city newspapers. *Barron's* also provides conversion tables on a weekly basis.

The exchange rates reported from these sources typically represent currency transfers by banks in amounts of $1 million or more at the time and date stated. The actual rates that applies to your exchange will therefore differ somewhat from the rates shown.

Exchange rates are presented in two ways, in terms of U.S. dollar equivalents (the U.S. dollar value of one unit of the foreign currency) and the foreign currency value per U.S. dollar (how much of the foreign currency one dollar can buy). The following example illustrates the format of an exchange table.

	U. S. Dollar Equivalent	Currency per U. S. Dollar
Britain (Pound)	1.9575	.5109

The U.S. dollar equivalent information is of major use to U.S. investors. For example, the table shows the British Pound to have a value of 1.9575. To buy one British pound will therefore cost $1.96. Ten pounds will cost $19.58, and 100 British pounds will cost $195.75. If, over time, the number shown goes down, that means the foreign currency is "cheaper" just as a camera is less expensive as its marked price falls. When the U.S. dollar is said to strengthen against a foreign currency, this means that the purchase price of that currency has been reduced. A given amount of U.S. dollars can therefore buy more of the foreign currency.

The column to the right on the British pound example rate chart displays the same data but from the other point of view—the cost of one dollar in terms of the foreign currency. In the case of the British Pound, the table shows that one dollar costs .5109 Pounds. Ten dollars therefore costs 5.109 Pounds and one-hundred dollars costs 51.09 Pounds.

Exchange rate tables can become confusing when the value of a single unit of two currencies differs greatly. As an example, if we look at the Italian Lira we can see that its exchange rate is very small in terms of the U.S. dollar equivalent.

	U. S. Dollar Equivalent	Currency per U. S. Dollar
Italy (Lira)	.0008807	1135.51

As with the British Pound interpretation, this number means that it takes that many dollars to buy one currency unit (in this case, a Lira). Ten Lira therefore costs .008807 U.S. Dollars, one-hundred Lira costs .08807 dollars (slightly less than nine cents!) and one-thousand Lira costs .8807 Dollars (about eighty- eight cents). As you can imagine, almost everyone in Italy is a millionaire in their domestic currency. For a foreigner it can be very easy to miscalculate or miscount a zero or two, with dire consequences possibly resulting.

CALCULATING THE COST OF A FOREIGN SECURITY

As an example, suppose you wish to buy 100 shares of a U.K. stock selling for 12.50 Pounds. The exchange rate (from the British pound example) is 1.9479, therefore the total cost is:

(12.5 Pounds/share) x (1.9575 Dollars/Pound) = $24.47/share
For one-hundred shares; $24.35 x 100 = $2,447

CALCULATING THE NUMBER OF FOREIGN SHARES THAT CAN BE PURCHASED

Let us suppose that you have $15,000 that you wish to use to purchase the same U.K. stock used in the example above. How many shares could you buy?

The exchange rate example shows .5109 Pounds per dollar. If you have $15,000, this is the equivalent of .5109 x 15,000 = 7663.50 Pounds. Since each share of stock is 12.50 pounds, we simply divide to determine how many shares can be purchased.

(7663.50 pounds)/(12.50 pounds/share) = 613.08 shares

NON-U.S. DOLLAR CALCULATIONS

The Wall Street Journal publishes a currency cross-rates table that can be used to price securities in any of the currencies listed. The information is presented in a matrix form. To find out how many units of currency A it takes to buy currency B, find country A on the vertical list and go across to the column of country B. The intersection provides the desired exchange rate.

For example, assume the table shows that one German Mark can purchase 1.09349 Canadian dollars. This information can be used in the same way as previously discussed. For instance, suppose a Ger-

German stock is trading at 45 Marks and you would like to know the value of 100 shares in Canadian Dollars.

100 shares x 45 Marks = 4500 Marks
Canadian Dollars per Mark = 1.09349
4500 Marks x 1.09349 = 4920.71 Canadian Dollars

Embassies of Major Countries

Argentina
1600 New Hampshire Ave., N.W.
Washington, D.C. 20009
(202) 939-6400

Australia
1601 Massachusetts Ave., N.W.
Washington, D.C. 20036
(202) 797-3000

Austria
2343 Massachusetts Ave., N.W.
Washington, D.C. 20008
(202) 483-4474

Bahamas
600 New Hampshire N.W. #865
Washington, D.C. 20037
(202) 944-3390

Belgium
3330 Garfield St. N.W.
Washington, D.C. 20008
(202) 333-6900

Bolivia
3014 Massachusetts Ave. N.W.
Washington, D.C. 20008
(202) 483-4410

Myanmar (Burma)
2300 S St. N.W.
Washington, D.C. 20008
(202) 332-9044

Canada
501 Pennsylvania Ave. N.W.
Washington, D.C. 20001
(202) 682-1740

Chile
1732 Massachusetts Ave. N.W.
Washington, D.C. 20036
(202) 785-1746

People's Republic of China
2300 Connecticut Ave. N.W.
Washington, D.C. 20008
(202) 328-2500

Colombia
2118 Leroy Pl. N.W.
Washington, D.C. 20008
(202) 387-8338

Costa Rica
1825 Connecticut Ave. N.W. #211
Washington, D.C. 20009
(202) 234-2945

Czechoslovakia (Czech and Slovak Federal Republic)
3900 Linnean Ave. N.W.
Washington, D.C. 20008
(202) 363-6315

Denmark
3200 Whitehaven St. N.W.
Washington, D.C. 20008
(202) 234-4300

Dominican Republic
1715 22nd St. N.W.
Washington, D.C. 20008
(202) 332-6280

Ecuador
2535 15th St. N.W.
Washington, D.C. 20009
(202) 234-7200

Egypt
2310 Decauter Pl. N.W.
Washington, D.C. 20008
(202) 232-5400

Finland
3216 New Mexico Ave. N.W.
Washington, D.C. 20016
(202) 363-2430

France
4101 Reservoir Rd. N.W.
Washington, D.C. 20007
(202) 944-6000

Germany
4645 Reservoir Rd. N.W.
Washington, D.C. 20007
(202) 298-4000

Greece
2221 Massachusetts Ave. N.W.
Washington, D.C. 20008
(202) 667-3168

Honduras
3007 Tilden St. N.W.
Washington, D.C. 20008
(202) 966-7702

Hungary
9310 Shoemaker St. N.W.
Washington, D.C. 20008
(202) 362-6730

Iceland
2022 Connecticut Ave. N.W.
Washington, D.C. 20008
(202) 265-6653

India
2107 Massachusetts Ave. N.W.
Washington, D.C. 20008
(202) 939-7000

Indonesia
2020 Massachusetts, Ave. N.W.
Washington, D.C. 20036
(202) 775-5200

Ireland
2234 Massachusetts Ave. N.W.
Washington, D.C. 20008
(202) 462-3939

Israel
3514 International Drive N.W.
Washington, D.C. 20008
(202) 364-5500

Italy
1601 Fuller St. N.W.
Washington, D.C. 20009
(202) 328-5500

Japan
2520 Massachusetts Ave. N.W.
Washington, D.C. 20008
(202) 939-6700

Korea
2370 Massachusetts Ave. N.W.
Washington, D.C. 20008
(202) 939-5600

Luxembourg
2200 Massachusetts Ave. N.W.
Washington, D.C. 20008
(202) 265-4171

Malaysia
2401 Massachusetts Ave. N.W.
Washington, D.C. 20008
(202) 328-2700

Mexico
1911 Pennsylvania Ave. N.W.
Washington, D.C. 20006
(202) 728-1600

Netherlands
4200 Linnean Ave. N.W.
Washington, D.C. 20008
(202) 244-5300

New Zealand
37 Observatory Circle N.W.
Washington, D.C. 20008
(202) 328-4800

Norway
2720 34th Street N.W.
Washington, D.C. 20008
(202) 333-6000

Pakistan
2315 Massachusetts Ave. N.W.
Washington, D.C. 20008
(202) 939-6200

Panama
2862 McGill Terrace N.W.
Washington, D.C. 20008
(202) 483-1407

Paraguay
2400 Massachusetts Ave. N.W.
Washington, D.C. 20008
(202) 483-6960

Peru
1700 Massachusetts Ave. N.W.
Washington, D.C. 20036
(202) 833-9860

Philippines
1617 Massachusetts Ave. N.W.
Washington, D.C. 20036
(202) 483-1414

Poland
2640 16th St. N.W.
Washington, D.C. 20009
(202) 234-3800

Portugal
2125 Kalorama Rd. N.W.
Washington, D.C. 20008
(202) 328-8610

Saudi Arabia
601 New Hampshire Ave. N.W.
Washington, D.C. 20037
(202) 342-3800

Singapore
1824 R St. N.W.
Washington, D.C. 20009
(202) 667-7555

South Africa
3051 Massachusetts Ave. N.W.
Washington, D.C. 20008
(202) 232-4400

Spain
2700 15th St. N.W.
Washington, D.C. 20009
(202) 265-0190

Sweden
600 New Hampshire Ave. N.W. # 1200
Washington, D.C. 20037
(202) 944-5600

Switzerland
2900 Cathedral Ave. N.W.
Washington, D.C. 20008
(202) 745-7900

Taiwan
Coordination Council for North American Affairs
555 Montgomery St. #501
San Francisco, CA 94111
(415) 362-7680

Thailand
2300 Kalorama Rd. N.W.
Washington, D.C. 20008
(202) 483-7200

Turkey
1714 Massachusetts Ave. N.W.
Washington, D.C. 20008
(202) 659-8200

U.S.S.R.
1125 16th St. N.W.
Washington, D.C. 20036
(202) 628-7551

United Kingdom
3100 Massachusetts Ave. N.W.
Washington, D.C. 20008
(202) 462-1340

Uruguay
1918 F. St. N.W.
Washington, D.C. 20006
(202) 331-1313

Venezuela
1099 30th St. N.W.
Washington, D.C. 20007
(202) 342-2214

Yugoslavia
2410 California St. N.W.
Washington, D.C. 20008
(202) 462-6566

INDEX

A

American banks: and banking services, 72-73; and foreign currencies, 73

American Depository Receipts (ADR's): and Asian Pacific Rim, 102; defined, 26; and economic modeling, 193; in Scandinavia, 150; inSwitzerland, 143; in U.K., 139

Asian Pacific Rim. *See* Super Region II

Asset allocation: defined, 171; equal allocation strategies, 172-75; and interest rates, 177-79; investor selected strategies, 195-76; trend reversal strategies, 180-83; variable allocation strategies, 17

B

Banks. *See* American banks, foreign banks, overseas banks, overseas banking services

Bonds: and economic modeling, 193; and timing models, 212- 13

C

Canada: and diversification, 85-86; investment opportunities, 88-90; and mutual funds, 90; and U.S. trade, 88-90

Common market. *See* European Community (EC)

Computer on-line services: Canadian Database, 45; Dow Jones International News, 42; and Dow Jones News, 42-43; and INVEST Database,45-44; and KYOTDO Database, 44-45

Currency exchange: calculating costs, 247; rates of, 245-46

D

Dollar averaging: defined, 157; philosophy of, 158; reverse averaging, 164,166; strategies, 159-63

Donoghue, W.E.: and interest rate allocation strategy, 177-79

E

Eastern Europe: economy of, 150-52; problems in, 153

Economic Modeling: and bonds, 193; and business cycles, 186-89, 194-96; and composite models, 209-14; and stocks, 190-93; and technical models,196-209

European Community (EC), 146-47; history of, 152-54; members, 153

F

Favored banking centers, 64-72

Financial inventories, 5

Financial privacy: and foreign bank accounts, 52-53, 57

Foreign banks: Austria, 66-67; Cayman Islands, 71-72; Hong Kong, 69-70; Singapore, 70-71; Switzerland, 65-66; U.K., 67-68. *See also* Overseas bank accounts, Overseas bank services

257